A Stor

My adventures and misadventures on the Camino del Norte, Camino Lebaniego and Camino de Finisterre

Stefan-Iulian Tesoi

Table of Contents

Day 30, 20 May, Baamonde
Day 31, 21 May, Sobrado
Day 32, 22 May, Arzua
Day 33, 23 May, Pedrouzo
Day 34, 24 May, Santiago De Compostela
Day 35, 25 May, Negreira
Days 36 & 37, 26 & 27 May, Cee & Finisterre

Day 1, 21 April - San Sebastian

I'm taking notes on the beautiful Ulia hill from the veranda of the Ulia youth hostel (it doesn't look like an albergue).

It was a really tough hike up here – with a backpack and a bag of food to carry on top – following a middle aged guy that was walking at a forced march pace and saying to keep up with him. He wasn't carrying anything, only his weight. He asked me something about the program, the program of the abuela or the albergue or something like that (what program??). On the sweaty 20 minutes forced march – I even had to do a short jog in order to catch up with him – he said that he wasn't sure if the place is an albergue or not; I wanted to swear at him and to abandon the the madness of following him into the unknown.

I finally get to the Ulia hostel which is right on top of the hill. The place that I've got to stay in is as big as an 1 room apartment or even bigger. I can't complain, I wanted to stay cheap and sleep away the night at the beach, on the sand or in some kind of shelter that I spotted beneath a shack advertising surf lessons. It was kinda rainy (weird weather here, windy, sunny and rainy, all at the same time). I didn't wanted to spend another cold, wet and sleepless night as I spent in Madrid. I totally underestimated the weather in Madrid. At 4 something in the morning there were 5 Celsius degrees, one hour earlier I think it felt like it was even less due to the relentless chilly wind. At some point I had the impression that I see and feel falling on me rain mixed with snow pouring in a sludge. For some reason, I wasn't surprised if it started to snow because all of the conditions seemed to be met in order for it to happen. My life got used in a weird sort of way to experiencing weird sorts of ways. I'm pushing myself to do this stuff and to get out of my comfort zone, to rewire my brain, to become a go-getter, all-in risk fiend, instead of being a time wasting, undecided fiend. But for now lets not go that far into my motives for doing this journey.

Something cool and interesting that I experimented today was when I asked an older lady walking a dog on a leash on the side of the picturesque river Almura, "Where is the albergue for Peregrinos in San Sebastian?". Actually I tried asking her in my Spanish: "Hola, usted sabe donde esta la albergue por peregrinos in San Sebastian?". For the rest of the journey I will be mixing Spanish with English, a bit of French and even Romanian in my attempts to communicate with the natives. She didn't knew the answer but she then asked another young man wearing headphones and sporty looking clothes, he also didn't knew so he asked another woman passing by, and then a white haired man passed by and was also asked; I was between wonder and puzzlement. I was wondering at the nice human gesture of helping – colaborativo style – a peregrino, even a fake one like me. I was puzzled by the fact that no one knew the answer. The young man finally got the location of the albergue by googling it and finding that it's on Ulia mountain street so he concluded that if I go in the direction of the mountain I will be able to find it. The older woman and the boy pointed me towards the direction: "follow the street until you get at that big, square building and than follow the beach to the right". I said that it made sense and being forever grateful I said muchas gracias to the lady and shook hands with the boy. Knowing a bit of broken Spanish, I felt elated and confident walking among my other fellow foreign and non-Spanish speaking peregrinos. I felt that I had a power that I could use to solve problems that others couldn't. Delighted to reach the beach and thus see for the first time the Atlantic, I followed the beautiful promenade and also took a few pics of the old style buildings and of something that looked like a statue of Columbus on top of a hill-cliff which is quite imposing – I concluded that is Columbus after its appearance and from the name of the street, Ana, one of the three boats that took Columbus on distant waters an shores.

At the beach I sat a bit on some kind of metal pipe partially covered by sand and looked at the ocean, the waves, at the surfers. The thought of staying a bit more in San Sebastian to learn to surf occurred to me. Watching all the people walking their dogs on the beach made me conclude that the beach is actually a poo heaven. I was sitting and trying to gobble down some food and to become one with the ocean and the universe by having some kind of a deep experience and profound thoughts. However, no deep experience or profound thoughts came towards my way; it was only the whiff of dog poo that came.

From what I've noticed, the people in San Sebastian are the most sporty citizens per capita from any town I've been to. Lots of runners doing their running along the river, along the promenade, on the beach, and even on this steep hill on the top of which I am standing now and writing these very words. I also noticed plenty of cyclists and a handful of surfers. Mix in the foreign people carrying their backpacks and wandering the streets and the town inspires a strong feeling of dynamism and action. The old architecture and the rustic appearance of the houses mixes greatly with this youthful dynamism. San Sebastian is not a town for a harried, tired, heavy backpack carrying traveler like me.

The Ulia "mountain" hill has the most insidious shape ever, it doesn't seem tall and it has a top which is hidden and out of sight from the bottom of the hill; you are made to think that you will reach the top at the next curb only to find that you have yet one more stretch of road until you hit another curb and so on.

At the end of the day, my hips show some bruises after I tried to put as much of the weight of the backpack on them by tightening the backpack's belt around my waist. My upper trapezoid muscles are also quite hit. My muscles are already starting to show signs of stress after a marathon of walking through Madrid and a forced march up the hill in San Sebastian.

Let's see what we've got at the end of day 1:

1 500 gr. Bag of mixed dried fruits (plums, apples, peaches, pears) + a bit of another bag left.

1 150 gr. Bag of roasted and salted cashews.

1 300 gr. Bag of Harribo gum bears – about half eaten.

1 200 gr. Bag of whole almonds.
6 63 gr. Lion bars.

In Madrid, I remember:

Seeing a runner at about five in the morning carrying a small backpack and slowly jogging across plaza Marcel.

Seeing the local police opening the park that has the Evita Peron memorial statue.

Observing people from a bench in a small park close to the Nuevos Ministerios subway exit on Orense. People looked calm, each one of them seemed to know what they had to do that day – unlike me.

People looked smartly and professionally dressed (there was a visible Zara Home sign that I could notice from across the small park, maybe it's the headquarters?).

A chill got into my bones as I sat there on the park bench trying to eat some food – gummy bears and a mix of dried fruits. I had to warm up by walking up and down the street in order to avoid hypothermia even though I was already tired from about eight and a half hours of walking since midnight and wandering on the streets of Madrid.

It's at night when the Spanish people respect the red and green colors of the traffic signs; when the working hours are slowly creeping in the morning, this fragile discipline seems to give way to hurriedness.

I noticed plenty of Fruteiras and "Verdadeiras"

(don't know if it's the correct name)? shops in Madrid. Bananas – 1 Euro, naranjas – 0.84 Euro, strawberries - 2.50 Euro/caja.

When asked where I am from I would say: "Romania", "România" and they would respond "Rumania? A...". I'm not sure how to interpret this A. Didn't sounded like an A as in "I'm A...mazed". It was more like a stereotyping, cataloging type of A.

I reserved a place on a car going to San Sebastian some days ago using the Spanish version of the BlaBlaCar site. The driver, Rene, a German living in Spain turned out to be friendly and a nice guy. I waited for the car somewhere around Nuevos Ministerios, at the Orense subway exit and we took off to San Sebastian soon after 10 AM.

On the Madrid-San Sebastian route: never ending series of hills with lush green grass, with orange and sometimes yellowish limestone rock, with snow capped peaks and hills further north.

Lots of - jumping deers – traffic warning signs. I haven't seen any deer but this might also be because of the fact that my eyes were shutting down despite my best efforts.

Great vasts of land empty of the presence of man. I was thinking that in the same conditions, in Romania there would have been lots of houses, annexes, yards, fences – all at the margin of the road.

I really like the stone and mortar types of houses and iglesias and the small, pastoral villages formed by them. It seems as nothing has changed since the era of Don Quijote de la Mancha. Even the windmills have a continued existence and presence in the form of modern eolian towers.

Day 1 costs

2.5   Euros at a Dealz shop: 2 1liter water bottles
       + 1 can of Original Pringles
2.5   Euros spent at a Cafeteria and Coffee shop
       on a chocolate muffin.
16.80 Euros: stay at the youth hostel Ulia.

Day 2, 22 April, Getaria

Got up at 7:19 AM, awaken up by my neighbors. Got my Magnesium and Spirulina pills, washed a bit, packed my clothes. I check out from the hostel and proceed into my adventure.

There is drinkable water from a pipe after the '8.5 km left to go until to Orosia' sign.

It's 12 PM and it had passed almost 4 hours since I left the hostel. I'm resting a bit in the middle of the forest at a source of potable water that runs from a hose with variable pressure. Eating almonds. Dropped 1l of water. Had to go to the bathroom in a place nearby – I'm not the first one to do it there. Being passed by other people.

Little break at Saint Martin's chapel. It's 14:00 PM

now and I've covered almost 18 kilometers + a few kilometers across San Sebastian. I feel like I can do the remaining 5.8 km to Zarautz in under six hours – I think that most of the albergues close at 8 PM. As I am writing, I was passed by someone again. Same person. The woman said Hi! and smiled. It seems that she doesn't takes breaks.

It's 15:26 PM and I'm sitting on a bench located maybe halfway down the hill (a hill full with wine vines) and Zarautz. I can see on top of the hill the camping site that was advertised on a sign I passed by. At that crossroad where I saw the sign I was faced with two options: to go inland for 1.8 km and reach Zarautz or to go somewhere on the right and go for another 2.2 km that would take me, as the sign said, about one hour. I was a bit puzzled by this sign and finally decided to go with the shorter route. Now sitting here on this bench I have a stunning view of the bay, the beach and the ocean. In the hillside I can also see steps going down the cliff and continuing to the beach bellow through some kind of bridge surrounded by fences on both sides. Most probably that is the longer but scenic detour and now I kinda regret not taking it. I see plenty of people going through the bridge on the beach and on the green pasture behind the bridge. The camping site looks quite full; there are plenty of cars passing on the little paved road behind my bench. To my left, looking downward, there is the little town of Zarautz with its buildings covered by orangish roof titles glistening in the sun. A sea of orange.

Checking out my Gronze printed pages which

contain all kinds of information, I realize that the objective of doing 40 km+ a day is not a reasonable objective; today's stage from San Sebastian is presented as a 22 km long distance and a 5h 30' long journey but it took me more than 5h30' to get to this point and I'm still not even in Zarautz yet. I also have to count in the fact that I'm trying to document this journey with pics and words along the way and to also take the time to enjoy and breath in the experience and the new places.

At about 17:45 PM I get to the Kenpaia Albergue after a steep climb through the little town of Getaria and after losing track of the yellow arrow signs that indicate the Camino. It's 12 Euros for 'hosting'. At the entry gates of the albergue a stench of smelly shit greets you. The smell persists even in the building. The beds are almost all occupied. Where all these people came from??? I haven't seen them on the road. Most of the people that I'm seeing now in the albergue are old. They look like they got here straight from the city, they don't look like backpackers. Two old Swedish people, a couple, are staying in the veranda room which also can double as a dinning room and reading some books. I guess that all the missing people, the occupants of the beds that I'm not seeing around the albergue are wandering around in the little fishing settlement bellow, maybe in the old city center with its old looking houses, old church and narrow streets paved with rocks. I skipped visiting it since I was too busy trying to find some kind of accommodation and calling it a day. I guess that they have the spare energy that I don't.

Pesky little flies keep bothering me. I don't usually

get bothered that easily but it's adding up: the flies, the people which are peregrinos more or less, the long arduous road, my aching back and feet. And there is also the shit that is spread along the pathway not far away from where I'm staying (in some kind of small, minimal, straw chair which rocks a bit) inside the dinning room. I'm pretty sure that's not horse manure and neither dog or cat scat and judging by its smell, consistency and size it could pass the human test. But enough with this place.

This is some other stuff that I've done today:

I checked out of the Ulia hostel. I asked the lady there if they have a peregrino passport and she said no, maybe I should try at a hostel that was situated in the other side of the town, close to Monte Igeldo and pointed the location on the map. I also asked her where the Camino starts, she said: "Camino de Santiago?" "Si", said that I should go about 50 meters from the entrance of the hostel through the parking lot and then go left. I followed her instructions and arrived at some kind of crossroad with many dirt paths pointing in various directions. I took the path that looked like the right one thinking that is very similar to the ones I'm used too in my hikes on the Bucium hills surrounding my hometown. I walk for a couple of meters and lo and behold I see an unexpected site! My first Camino De Santiago sign! I must admit that the sign looked pretty cool, it looked like a moss covered old piece of stone carved and painted with bright yellow. The bright yellow arrow would be the first one in a long row of arrow signs that I would be looking for and following all day long. The forest path looked really cool with its luxuriant ferns, green lush vegetation, palm trees and vines. It looked like I took a leap in time too, I wouldn't have been surprised if some prehistoric creature jumped out of the trees. On the track I soon began to see other travelers and runners. At some point out of nowhere a girl that I had the impression that I've seen before (maybe I've seen her in San Sebastian the day before?) passed by me running and mumbling something that I didn't understand, I don't remember replying. Soon after that encounter I noticed that I have a big bulge in my pocket; it was a bag of gum bears sticking out of the pocket of my jacket. That bag of gummy bears and then later on, a bag of dried fruits were to be my breakfast.

The climb down the hill was very pleasant and frankly if all the journey would have been through this kind of terrain it would have been extraordinary. On some steep portions of the hill I started to do a little jog in order to use the gravity and momentum to gain some speed and time and to conserve some energy. Plenty of other joggers on the road. At some point two girls walking their two dogs passed by me on the road. One of the dogs, Google, went crazy and went off the path and into the 'jungle'. One of the girls kept shouting "Gooogle! Gooogle! Gooogle!" Soon I intersected the path that I climbed on the day before; I am reminded about the sneezing little goat that I saw yesterday when I passed by a building which seemed to be some kind of farm with little pygmy goats around it. Going further down the hill and entering the canopy of buildings, all very chic, white and sea resort looking I realized that

that I haven't noticed all the yellow Camino signs that were plastered on circulation signs, walls and on the pavement. Surely I must have passed by enough of them. I notice a church but it's closed. I continue my journey following the arrows this time and going back through places that I've already been through. The arrows take me through the center of the city, an area that I had some regrets for not checking it out in more depth. Going through the city, it disappointed me, au contraire, old buildings mixing up with new, modern buildings, businesses just opening up, working people going about their ways, tourists with chic and a bit sporty looking clothes strolling up and down the narrow streets and promenades. I stop at an tourism information center and ask if they have passports for peregrinos. The answer is no and the lady there pointed on the map the closed church that I noticed earlier, there might be the possibility that they have passports there. She also said that the church opens at 10 AM. No way I'm going back to the church and waiting until 10 AM. "Some location closer to this part of the town?" - I am asking and pointing to the left side of the map. She points back at the location of a hostel situated in the other part of the city so finding that hostel becomes my main mission. Onward we go! I'm making sure that I keep on munching on dried fruits to fuel me, I've already killed off the gummy bears since a long time ago. Going on the boardwalk type of promenade close to the beach I keep seeing people running, people walking, some of them at a fast pace, there are lots and lots of them – it wasn't a comfortable sight and feeling that it generated for me, people were usually staring at me. Their dynamism was also bringing up the competitiveness in me.

The map that I got from the hostel the day before proved to be really useful to my mission since I've lost track of the markings at some point and because I had the impression that locating the hostel would mean that I would have to go off route. I passed by an interesting and exotic looking garden with baobab looking type of trees with no leaves and with root looking type of branches. They don't make an ecstatic site to see in my opinion, they only look weird and it's weird seeing them in such a resort type of city like San Sebastian. I keep on looking for signs and go on what seems like the last street in San Sebastian, located at the very border of the city, at the foothill of Mount Igeldo. Walking up the street I begin to notice the yellow signs again. At some point at a crossroad the yellow sign was pointing to the right but the location of the hostel on the map as pointed out by the receptionist was straight ahead and up the hill. I go on a detour from the official Camino path and I suddenly notice an old lady, about 20 meters up on the road, looking in my direction and making sleep gestures, folding her hands under her head. I wanted now to go right and start climbing on the 'mountain' but I kept looking at the old lady and she was frantically making the same gesture again and again. I thought that she was paid by some hostel to do some kind of gimmick advertising. "Interesting advertising" I thought, "out of the box thinking". Then another thought crossed my mind: what if she is actually pointing at the hostel that I'm looking for? I begin walking towards her and soon realized that her nonverbal communication was actually directed towards me and not to the car and people traffic on the road. "Camino? Camino de Santiago" "Si" I reply. She started speaking in Spanish and from my understanding I think that she kept saying that there is a location further up the road for pilgrims. "Pasaporte por peregrinos?" I ask, "Si". The woman understood that I also understood her Spanish so with this tacit mutual understanding our conversation ended. I thank her. I follow her directions and soon enough I am greeted with the view of the hostel that I've been looking for. I enter full of hope and find a young man talking on the phone. I wait until he finishes. "Passports for peregrinos?" "Si" and he goes on to search for them. He finds them and gives me some kind of form and the passport, tells me how to fill them in. I fill them in as best as I can and ask what to write in the organization field. Well, it seems that I'm now in an organization called Amigos del Camino de Santiago. He applies my first stamp on the passport and I am elated "The first one! And many more to come!". I ask how much does it cost. "Nothing". Great!

My official Camino journey has just started. I go back down the road enthusiastic due to completing my mission and due to the fact that the passport didn't cost me anything. Near Marbil, my new journey starts with a steep climb up the Monte Igeldo. I am reminded of yesterday's tough walk and that this is no easy business. Strolling across the town for a few clicks was a piece of cake. At some point, in an opening in the green walk on the side of the narrow path, I get a glimpse of the upcoming scenery: green hills and a lot of up and down climbing. At some point I pass by a small cluster of bamboo which made for an interesting site for me. I don't think that I had the opportunity before to see bamboo. Not long after, I see on the side of the road a raincoat, it looked quite heavy and thought that maybe a peregrino ditched it in order to get rid off some ballast. Or maybe some peregrino who is returning back from Santiago and doing the reverse journey ditched it as some kind of "fuck it!" gesture. "Evrika!"

Day 3, 23 April, Izarbide

I wake up at about 5:30 AM; had about six hours of sleep. There was a lot of snoring going on in the room. It was hard to get to sleep but the tiredness finally prevailed. From now on I will be wearing ear plugs in hostels, I didn't wear them last night because I didn't wanted to bother my neighbor which was sitting one level below me in the bunk bed and who already went to sleep while I was busy taking today's notes; plus, I didn't really felt like going treasure hunting in my backpack.

People are already starting to get up. Phones and little pocket lights are starting to get lit and the bathroom to get used. I have a breakfast consisting in magnesium and Spirulina pills downed with a little bit of water, a Lion bar and a handful of almonds. I plan to stack a bag of dried fruits in my jacket to munch later on while being on the road. I don't think that I have eaten well enough yesterday and drank enough water, I noticed this morning that my pee has a darker color than it usually does which is a sign of dehydration.

I installed last night a simple notepad app on my phone, this way I should be able to take notes more easily while I am walking, no more stopping and reaching out for my notebook and pen. I leave the albergue at 7:10 AM. The walk soon transforms into a king of the hill competition as I am trying to pass other walkers who are also climbing the steep hill. They take a short break, turn back and wave at me.

I go through a small eucalyptus forest and a vineyard, the smell is lovely...lavender I think. Now it smells like pine trees. Basque runners are coming from the opposite direction. In front of me there is a large opening with the ocean in full view.

I pass two gentlemen walkers while running down a steep side of the hill towards a city. A few hundred meters after, it's their turn to pass me. The competition is on! Marrina Berri...I guess that Berri means restaurant in the local language, I have seen this word before. A Spanish looking dog, dogs tend to look like their owners isn't it? There are a lot of funny pictures on the Internet with pets that look like their owners and there is even one BBC article claiming that this phenomenon is a "scientific" fact. I hear teenagers talking about cosplay. There is some kind of a monument dedicated to runners; it's located in a small park and is surrounded by benches. A cannon.

Ahead of me I have my two scouts leading the way. This way I don't have to look for arrows and other Camino symbols. My scouts just took a wrong turn. I will have to start eating some proper food given all of this steep climbing, otherwise my energy levels will go down and my muscles will begin to shut down.

I have a little chat with one of the French guys – my scouts – while climbing a steep hill full of vineyards and pastoral land. When there are steep downhill portions of paved roads I prefer to run so this is what I have done for about one kilometer until I get to a crossroad. I buy a bottle of homemade cider from a farm. It costs me 2.5 Euros, "drink it here or take the bottle" says the sign at the little unmanned booth. You have to put the money in a glass jar and there are already a few Euros in it. I like the fact that this selling process is based on trust. There is also some kind of bees wax product available for sale. I sip a bit and take the bottle. The drink has some alcohol content in it, it tastes a bit sweet, a bit of apples, it's not bad.

The first stop of the day is somewhere near a building that has a huge parrot drawn on it. The parrot says "Haz da!". It's 10:46 AM. I've been walking like a fiend, passing most of the peregrinos that went out of the albergue earlier than me. I eat dried fruits and drink the apple cider to get some energy. I should be close to Zumaia by now. I'm at the entrance of a village or a small town and I have no idea what it's called. The short-haired and boyish looking girl that I've seen yesterday passes me. Her grimaces tells me that she is in pain. I notice hoards of cyclists as I look down the highway. Running, cycling, walking, being active seems to be some sort of religion around these parts, sports are practiced regularly and by large numbers of people.

I realize that I'm actually somewhere close to Itziar...I check my map and also see a sign marked Itziar. In my scramble of walking unending series of steep hills I completely lost my sense of location. The names of the places are so bizarre and uncommon for me that it's hard to keep track of them. I have a short conversation with Niels from Denmark. He thought that I am Peter from Czech Republic. It started to rain so it's time to start moving again. I find a little shop somewhere in the village and I buy 1 long baguette, 1 bag of Dorittos and two Filipinos for 4.85 Euros. I'm a bit dizzy from drinking that bottle of cider.

I meet Niels again, he is taking pictures of cows and is heading in the opposite way. He says that the path I'm heading to it's not the right one. I'm pretty sure that I'm on the right track so I keep walking for a few meters more and see the yellow arrow. "Look Niels, it's the yellow arrow, we are on the right track". Niels seems confused.

It's 12:26 PM now and I'm somewhere down in the little city of Deba. Due to Niels and his guidebook we just take two elevators down to the bottom of the city thus sparring myself a lot of energy and time instead of taking the longer route down. We soon find the yellow arrows and cross the little city and its plaza. In the plaza there was some kind of event going on and some nice bagpipe music was echoing. Niels is gone looking to have lunch somewhere. I'm sitting on a bench with the Deba train station behind me. A lone passenger, a cyclist is waiting for his train. It's raining a bit. I notice Arabs and blacks wandering the streets. A black man in traditional clothes. A dog named burrito. I'm eating Dorritos and a damned dorrito pierces the gum of my teeth and remains stuck in.

I'm taking notes now in a bunk bed in a hostel called Izarbide. Got here more than an hour before, now it's 17:41 PM. Location: between Ermita del Calvario and Ibiri Auzoa, I guess. I've done 23 km today, more or less.

Took notes on my phone, last time in Deba. Since then I've been walking up a hill which has the word 'kalvar' in its name, a word that it's very similar to the English calvary. In Romanian calvar means pain, misery, sufferance. The climbing on the hill that greets you after exiting the little city of Deba was kalvarish indeed with a steep ascent through the forest. On top of the hill, after the ermita (church), the dirt road becomes a paved road. On the last length of today's stage I walked together with Niels the Dane. There where dark, menacing clouds moving quick towards us but luckily, not long after the church the welcoming site of the Izarbide albergue greeted us. Seeing the bar, which also doubles as a reception area, my first impression was that it was going to be a costly stay here. Turns out that staying over the night is 13 Euros which is not bad for the tired peregrino. Niels ended up paying 30 Euros for a bed, dinner and desayuno (breakfast). He initially thought that all of these would cost only 13 Euros, "great!" he said. He doesn't know much Spanish so he just said "Si" at everything the lady at the counter asked him, "You want this? Si. You want this? Si. OK, 30

Euros".

Niels is quite a character, he seems like a nice guy. He also takes notes along the journey and posts on his blog called Camino Mi Privio which is in Danish. Niels told me that he trained for this Camino by walking up and down 5-6 times the highest top in Denmark which is about 149 meters tall and also walking long distances on the beach, somewhere in the ranges of 38-50 km, said that it was rough doing that. I told him that I trained for the journey by running semi-marathons. He is well documented and told me about the Picos of Europa mountains which are also an objective of my trip. He told me about the Camino Lebaniego and about some route starting from Ceres, from my understanding it's a walk across a gorge where you have to be very careful where you step since there is the possibility of falling 10-20 meters down. Niels has a good walking speed and stamina, it might be all that speed walking training that he did for the past two weeks before jumping on the Camino.

Even though there is plenty of time left in the day, I decided to stop at Izarbide because the alternative would be to walk all the way to Markina which is about 19 km away, about a days' worth of walking. And no albergues or cheap alternatives until there from what I know. It's not a bad place here at the hostel, there is drinkable water, some amenities, there is a fireplace that spews smoke in the whole place so it smells of pine and smoke inside.

I have eaten almost all of the baguette that I was caring all the way from Itziar – it's a well traveled baguette, with half of a 120 gr. can of vegetal pâté. I had to leave some of the bread for tomorrow morning, otherwise I would have eaten all of it. While I was eating outside I saw the boyish looking girl that I have seen yesterday and today passing on the road. She didn't stopped to get a place as most of the other people did. I noticed that she had a small tattoo on her neck, bellow her ear.

Here at the hostel I'm keeping my activity at a minimum, I dozed a bit in the bed, covered in the makeshift blanket that I'm carrying with me so I can warm up. Luckily, my French neighbor carries around some kind of a heating device that is quite big to be carried – it's from Switzerland from my understanding, he discussed it with his friend in French – and he plugged it in for a while. He and his friend seems to be plotting some kind of operation, speaking in whispers, looking over guides and maps, saying things like "trucs" and "allemands", it seems like they will launch a blitzkrieg tomorrow and they seem confident about it. The Germans will never know what hit them. Here in the chicos room is quite a silence, I'm the youngest guy here, most of the people look over 50 years old but they seem to be fit for their age.

Day 4, 24 April, Zarautz

I wake up at 6:30 AM, people start moving headlamps and lights are glowing, some even left already. I finish my baguette and the rest of the vegetal pâté. Some people, including Niels, are waiting for the 7:30 AM breakfast. Eating my filipinos. Last night and maybe throughout the whole night it rained. Its quite cold. I leave at 7:55 AM in the rain.

Another day, another series of steep hills to climb, my backpack feels heavier and heavier. I'm breathing heavily and I resent the 1 kilogram of cans and half a kilo of papers that I'm carrying. I'm starting to think at the journey as a punishment even though the scenery is very beautiful.

No wonder that in Belgium there is still a law stating that once a year a prisoner is pardoned if he makes the pilgrimage (under a watchful eye of course).

I adjust my backpack on my hips by pulling the lower belt of the backpack tighter and remove my rain jacket that is making me sweaty. Things get a little bit better now.

I fill half a one liter bottle from a pipe located near a sign that says Arnoate. The water seems to be good for drinking even though some moss lives inside the pipe. No problem, the moss acts like a filter. By this time I realize that there is no point in carrying more than half a liter of water a time since there are plenty of water sources on the track and in villages and towns. I used to carry another one liter bottle but I ditched it the bin this morning.

Ten kilometers more to go until Markina. I get a very good phone signal on a hill, full bars, the best signal in days. I try to phone home but I don't have enough credit. BS I bought a brand new prepaid card. I notice two black Limax snails on the trails...hmm...a good source of proteins. A blaze seemed to have run through this clearing that reminds me of the Piatra Craiului Mountains. For some reason I'm humming an Araucana song called Quimey Neuquén by José Larralde.

The air is filled with the freshly mentholated smell of pines and eucalyptus. I arrive at a path made of sharp flint kind of rocks, rocks that look like they could have been used by the prehistoric ancestors of the Basques to make arrows. Last night it rained quite heavily so portions of the road are completely soaked up with water today. The advance is tough, I fear that if it keeps on raining like this I won't be able to continue because of all the mud. I'm thinking that I'm not the only person in this situation. If I would be doing this journey alone I would have questioned my mental sanity.

In Markina I ask a guy if he knows where I could buy some bread. "Donde puedo comprar pan?" he replied "pan? a cafeteria". It looks like a fancy and expensive cafeteria so I am a bit skeptical of going there so I start walking in the opposite direction but the guy insists that there is bread in there. I give it a try and I can see from outside that there was indeed bread inside – along with expensive pastries and fancy dressed people. I buy a bread for 1.3 Euros. Having a bread in my bag is making me more confident.

I arrive at the Zarautz monastery at 14:20 PM. First break of the day. 24 km done today. The monk says that the accommodation is donativo so I give him all my change from my pockets.

16:05 PM – I go to a place nearby the monastery where I order Bacalao fish and a pint of Amstel Redler beer. The fish is 5 Euros and the beer costs 2 Euros. The guy there "forgets" to give me the change from the 10 Euros bill that I give him and I also concluded that I've been given a special inflated price for the Bacalao, I never saw a menu. I buy from the monastery shop 1 kilogram of Udabeni honey (produced in a Cistercian monastery) for 8 Euros and a bottle of local monastery homemade beer (cerveza zioritza elaboration artesanal) for 4 Euros. Beer ingredients: agua, malta de cebada, cebada, lupulo, azucar, levadura. Made after an ancient recipe. The honey should give me lots of energy, it doesn't spoil and goes well on bread; plus it doesn't seem that expensive.

Niels finally arrives and he occupies the last of the eight places in the room. There is another room with eight places situated on a lower level. I go at the church at 7:30 PM for the Vesperas at Niels' suggestion. It is an interesting experience, the first one of this sort for me. I feel a sense of peacefulness. We have a pilgrims dinner at about 8:20 PM. We are served vegetarian soup because the monastic order is vegetarian from my understanding. Mushrooms, carrots, peas, noodles are some of the ingredients. At this point every calorie counts and since I arrived at the monastery I've been eating and drinking for much of the time. Soup, bread with pâté, bacalao fish and a beer at the bar, monastery beer - mine and others, cheese kudos to another roommate, John (he said: "I'm not carrying this tomorrow, you guys help me eat it") and finally soup again.

I have a series of interesting conversations with my roommates. John is from the States and did some Caminos before so he has a lot of experience. I learn a thing or two from him. If I learned something today it would be the fact that the human spirit prevails through adversity with determination and cohesion. John makes a proposal: everyone should get ingredients tomorrow from a supermarket in Gernika in order to make a nice dinner at the next albergue.

Day 5, 25 April, Eskerika

I wake up at about 5:50 AM. I slept pretty well and for this I have to thank my ear plugs - and to blame my fatigue. I dreamed about walking through towns together with other people and it's obvious that my dreams reflect what I've been doing for the past days. At some point in my dream, I pass by a house that has a huge dog. The fence to the house is open and the dog is unchained so I have to quickly close the fence to avoid being attacked by the dog. Weird dream.

It seems that I manage to lose my good writing pen and manage to break the tip of the second one so from now on I might be reduced to only writing on my phone. It's now 6:30 AM and my roommates are still in their beds, dozing off and recovering from yesterday's tough walk. I'm the youngest person here by a big margin. I think that the average age of my roommates is somewhere around 50 years. I remember what John told me yesterday, that he didn't saw many Romanians on the road, only two Romanian girls on the Camino Frances. Stories from John:

An Australian guy came for four weeks to do the Camino and to learn Spanish. He apparently managed to learn enough because, as John puts it, he understands about 60% of what he reads/listens. A German guy walked the Camino starting from the doorsteps of his house; he spoke only German, his son who came to pick him up spoke perfect English. We talked about languages and the fact that in large countries you don't necessarily have to learn other languages, in small ones like mine you have to. Talking about the Aragonese dialect John jokingly said that he liked coming to Spain because it seems like it's a country of which no one wants to be a part. "Spain is a big country formed from smaller countries that don't want to be part of Spain".

My roommates are quite well documented. they sit and talk about guides that they read, they are checking maps, forums and Xavier (one of the two French "scouts") even has a schedule nicely planned with locations, days and distances. John says that the German guide books are the best ones, they also contain terrain marks in case that someone gets lost. I leave the monastery at 7:50 AM.

I'm at the Eskerika albergue now.

I had a series of interesting conversations today. I spoke with Sofia from Holland, John and Chris from Canada and with Didier from France (the other French "scout") for a short while in Gernika. Today was hard to be alone since my steps intersected with theirs for so many times. I managed to drop my phone and this in turn affected its ability to take pics. When I'm trying to take a picture it shows Error: A SD card is needed yadda yadda yadda...so I didn't took pics today with my phone. I managed to fix the problem later on by opening up the phone, getting out the memory card and putting it back on.

I have seen two dying snakes on the road today. In Gernika I bought 2 long breads for 1.85 Euros, 3 bananas and 4 clementines for 3.85 Euros, Lays chips and some chocolate biscuits for 2.75 Euros. I need all the calories that I can get. I carried quite some weight in my bag and this really tired my hands since I'm carrying it with my hands and not on my back. In Gernika they were celebrating 79 years since they had been bombed by the Germans during the Spanish Civil War. What a celebration it must be! To celebrate the fact that you were bombed...Of course, there is the connection between Gernika and Pablo Picasso's Guernica famous painting.

A portion of the road looked like it was a rainforest: lush green, vines, big ferns, water running in small streams, trees covered with moss. A relic from Jurassic one might say. The portion outside Gernika was quite tough and it kept being that way all the ten kilometers to the albergue. Also, somewhere along the road a marshy portion was quite troublesome. I collected some red berries from that marsh, Chris says that they are from the rose hip plant.

We had to wait until 15:00 PM for the hostel to open. The south Korean guy that I've seen before on the road and in albergues got to the albergue with the hospitaleros car. He got out of the car like a boss, all smiles. He got completely lost and due to a fortunate turn of events he got picked up. Staying at the albergue costs 14 Euros and I've also bought a little can of beer for 1 Euro. I think that people are shooting guns here, I'm staying in the yard and I've heard shots twice already. There is a dog here named Lolita. The owners' name is Yachi. I'm using the Internet (which is not working that well) to do some research for the later stages of my trip. I have no idea when I'm coming back home. There is an airplane ticket from Vola for Lisbon-Bucharest at 70 euro. The price doesn't seem too bad.

Some newly come woman asks a puzzled Niels if she can do anything to be of help. Niels thinks about her offer for a while and says laundry. Funny guy.
There are two Italian guys who are making everyone laugh. One of them is Ciccio and I don't know the other one's name, lets call him Fellini. Fellini is bald but he is carrying a hair dryer with him. The girls in the albergue are laughing at him because of this but he is using the hair dryer to dry his shoes. "Who is laughing now?" he says.

Day 6, 26 April, Portugalete

I do like the Korean and wake up at 6:16 AM. I leave at 7:20 AM. At about 12 PM I finish my breakfast on a bench near a school located somewhere outside Bilbao. I did some shopping at a little supermarket in Bilbao and bought some tangerines, bananas, bread and sangria - Don Simon sangria "#1 sangria in the world" all for 4.85 Euros.

I arrived and checked in at the Bide Ona albergue in Portugalete after I got completely lost in Bilbao. John told me to get to the world renowned Guggenheim museum and from there to walk along the river. I did that. The problem was that I walked in the complete opposite way and ended up in the other side of Bilbao. I got to a small park and only when I asked a woman that was walking her dog for directions I realized that I'm totally lost; she showed me my current location on her mobile phone. She recommended me to take the metro to Portugalete (Eskizu station or something like that) and she walked a portion of the road to the station together with me. I took the metro to Portugalete and the cost was 1.85 Euros. It saved me a lot of headache and hustle. As soon as I got out from the train a woman approached me and I told her that I'm heading to an albergue. She asked which one so I checked one of my Gronze papers and showed her the name Bide Ona...she said aahhh...and guided me to the albergue which was not far away from the exit of the metro station.

I met here at the hostel friendly faces in the form of the two French. They also took the metro. Its not even 16:30 PM and I'm getting quite bored already....I've eaten plenty of food so I'm not hungry and I don't really have much to do besides writing. What to do? Go back to Bilbao with the metro and visit the city?

Checking my email I'm reminded of Goodreads; maybe I should start listening to an audiobook on my mp3 player, I have been carrying it so long for nothing. I go for a beer with Xavier. It seems that he is quite an accomplished runner. He is 63 years old and he's been running for 35 years, did 48 marathons including the New York, Berlin, London ones and the tough and prestigious Marathon des Sables which takes place in the Sahara desert. I went to the Puente Colgatiente with the gang...they wanted to go to a restaurant but I didn't so I tried to get back at the albergue but got kinda lost. Somehow I managed to get back. Had an interesting conversation with John on the way back. He also noticed the competitive nature of the French. He said he never saw something like this in his four Caminos.

Day 7, 27 April, Islares

It's night here in Islares and I just realized that I've lost my phone charger. From here on I'm back to doing my writing in the old pen and paper fashion. I'll have to get a phone charger in some bigger town.

Woke up quite early at about 5:16 AM and had to go to the bathroom. Last night all that sangria I've drink kinda went to my head, it has 7% alcohol content but it's 1.5 liters of it.

The first hour or so of walking was marked by rain - had to put my light raincoat on. The road passed through plenty of buzzing pylons caring electricity.

Today was a tough day. I did the 27 kilometers between Portugalete and Castres and the 9 kilometers from Castres to Islares. I walked across some amazing scenery close to the coast. The sand dunes and the beach after La Arena were amazing. Amazing was also the promenade that overlooked the beach and the ocean. Another great scenery was the one before entering Islares, jagged white rocks with trees growing between them. There was plenty of road today on highways or close to a highway. I took the N-643 highway whenever I could in order to use the straightest route.

Castres looks like a resort town; there are plenty of unpicked dog shits, my impression is that it's a town of snobs and I felt strange and a freak as a peregrino so I wanted to get out of that place as fast as possible. The albergue there is a small place with only 16 places so I did quite some scrambling (as per John's advice) to get there faster, I ran a few kilometers down the hill on the highway and passed in this process at least six German people. I passed near the albergue and took a peek inside and it looked deserted. In town I was interested in some sea food (5 euros for a little tray of shrimps) but ended up buying some fruits instead and some salchichon extra and two Oreos.

The albergue here costs only 5 Euros but its not anything special, no wifi, no breakfast...it looks like a former enfermeria. Kindergarden. We are 4 peregrinos here at this point: me, John, a girl from Germany who also listens to metal – she recognized my Burzum hoodie, and an Italian guy that I saw at the albergue in Portugalete.

I had a conversation with the German girl; she came from Castres and has some problems with her feet, stayed two days in Portugalete to recover, walked barefoot from Castres to here. She has a bachelor degree in Political Science and got an internship in political journalism (she starts in June), in May she has to attend her brother's wedding so that means that she can't do the whole Camino. She gave me an antiblister patch which I used.

Seemed to be bothered by the people coming in including the family from Switzerland of a father and his 3 sons. We talked about German guides, the Camino and religion.

Day 8, 28 April, Laredo

This day started a little bit early for me. It seems that Tino's (he's Italian) story about divorcing his wife and his son not speaking with him and the fact that he is doing the Camino for his 90+ years old mom struck a cord within me. I had a dream about me and my step-father. In the dream he was trying to explain to me his behavior. I felt quite unmoved by his arguments, I know that he is a superficial person and an ignorant. I woke up from the dream and started to think; I got quite emotional, when the Italian guy went to the bathroom I decided to get up and to go outside the albergue to think.

I felt the need to walk and to clear my mind. My conclusion was that I am better off alone, there is no need for me to insist where I'm not wanted. I was thinking at how these Spanish people were willing to help a foreigner; the woman in Bilbao that helped me even asked if I need any money, people help you even if you don't ask, but my own step-father is unwilling to help me in times of need. This thought makes me quite sad. I'm pretty much decided to interrupt my relation with this side of the family. I'm thinking that my step-siblings don't really show any interest in me. Every time I go there it seems like I have to force interactions; most of the time when I go there it seems like wasted time because I end up alone in the living room watching the TV, they don't come and ask me how I've been doing.

I went off to clear my head but I got stuck outside in the cold because I couldn't open the door that got locked after I closed it and I also didn't wanted to disturb the sleep of the occupants either. All of this lasted maybe two hours. They were two cold and miserable hours spent trying to keep myself warm. To my left I could see an ocean fleet and a clear sky, to my right I could see the moon shinning and slowly giving way to daylight. I wanted to go to the beach and see the sunrise but the sun didn't raised from the ocean horizon. Morning comes and I'm let in by some Spanish guy "llaves abajo" - apparently the keys were under the mat all this time.

On my way to Laredo I listened to Aziz Ansari and to George Carlin. I needed some uplifting. It seems that somehow I took a longer route since I found John ahead of me on the trail; he said that the Chilean girls that were last night at the albergue and who are traveling on their bikes passed him about a half an hour ago, I went ahead earlier then them and I never saw them pass me. I asked an old man that was using a scythe to cut grass if I'm on the right track but he ignored me completely even when I waved my hands at him, he didn't even looked at me.

Today's journey wasn't anything spectacular, I didn't liked the fact that I had to take a loop – an useless loop from the R-643 main road. However, I did walk on the beach in Laredo and it was an amazing experience: sun, waves and sand. I walked slowly across the sand.

I walked part of the journey with John but after stopping for water I remained behind and near a church he disappeared (my impression was that he accelerated his pace so that he can get rid of me, I don't know exactly why he would do that). He went on a road to the right, a local lady told me to go left. After climbing the hill in that direction I saw at some point a peregrino coming from behind that looked like John but I'm not sure if it was him. I guess that he eventually took the shortcut by following the R-634 main road. I kept looking backwards but I never saw him again.

In Laredo I asked people if they know where I can find a recarcador. I visited four shops, three of them were some kind of a Chinese bazaar, and a supermarket but it was no to avail since not one of the cables that I tried worked for my phone.

In the port I find out that the last ferry to Santona was at 14:30 PM. I had to turn back to Laredo and find accommodation. I get a ride from a construction worker named Pedro who said that he also did the Camino, the Castilla La Mancha Camino, in twelve days. He drove me to the Trinidad Albergue at which I am staying now.

I went to the supermarket and spent 9.15 Euros on: a 500 gr. Bread 0.75E, Queso Light 250 gr. - 2.05E, Chorizo Picante 280 gr. - 1.99E, Sandevid Limon juice – 1.33E, Tortillas Banderos 200gr. - 0.89E, Green Olives 380 gr. - 1.10E, Vino Fuente Vina Rosado – 0.99E. The supermarket chain is called Lupe. I ate and drank about half of all the stuff that I bought and now I am writing these lines with a full belly! I also used my wine opener for the first time.

Staying at the Albergue cost me 10 Euros.

I heard some French and familiar voices while eating, I rush out of my room and it turns out that Xavier, Didier and Sofia are also here; they were heading to the church. Xavier told me that they got lost and wandered clueless for about 10 km. Niels lost his watch. Xavier offered to help me but his phone cable didn't worked for my phone.

When you call at the Trinidad Albergue intercom you are greeted with Ave Maria, I didn't knew how to respond so I also said Ave. The nun at the desk kept saying "vale".

Day 9, 29 April, Guemes

Started the day having to go to the bath; I had no idea what hour it is. I looked through the little bathroom window and saw that it's still night so I decided to do some more sleeping. I finally woke up and didn't rushed knowing that the boat to Santona wouldn't leave until 9:00 AM. I figured that if I leave at about 8:00 I would have about an hour to reach the departing location which seemed doable (it's a four km long distance by my estimations). Not long after leaving Casa Trinidad, a church bell announced 8 o'clock. "Perfect" I thought.

Getting up I noticed something that looked like a boil on my hand – three of them – my first impression was that I was bitten by something but it didn't seemed probable, maybe it was bad hygiene or the food, I thought. I finished all the yesterdays' food that I bought from the supermarket, I skipped the 7:30 AM desayuno because I was full. Leaving the Casa Trinidad I noticed that there were only two pairs of boots left in the boots rack including mine. I thought that the others will get to the boat departure location sooner than they should and end up waiting there. I eventually got there within a few minutes from the boats' departure time. Traveling by boat was amazing, but the ride was so short that it took only about the time in which I ate a tangerine left from yesterday. By water, there are only about 600-700 meters that are separating Laredo and Santona, on land however, there are 18 kms.

An important note for today's journey would be the fact that between the beach in Laredo and the albergue here in Guemes I saw only one source of drinkable water and this source was a few hundred meters from the Abuelo Pedro Albergue. I made the mistake of not carrying any water with me. Luckily, I was well hydrated from yesterday when I drank water, 1.5l of juice, a bottle of wine and "drank" a bag of juicy tangerines that I bought for only 1 Euro. At some point, not knowing that I'm only about one km from getting to the albergue I had to ask an old man who was watering his garden for water. At some point in this deserted looking village (where are all the people?!) I passed by a place called "Food and Rock and Roll". It sounded very good and enticing but to my dismay I noticed that it's closed from Monday to Friday, it was only a small time kind of thing. There, in the courtyard, there was a girl working at what seemed to be her homework. I asked her: "Open?" "No...No", "Agua?" "No...No" shaking her head. "You little shit" I thought.

Today was quite sunny and hot and it made my decision of not carrying water even reckless. Today's road wasn't that difficult, it was mostly on flat ground around the Laredo beach, in Santona and in the M...(forgot the name) valley. I had to go uphill on a detour from the main highway and in some two other parts of the road. The lack of difficulty was compensated by the distance, after my estimations, I did about 28 kilometers. For the last kilometers I was quite dismayed because I didn't saw any signs, I had no idea where I was and how much I had left, the lack of water, the lack of people in the little villages and places that I was going through. Guemes seemed to never come.

I had a conversation with the German mother and daughter team while walking through Santona and then out of it; we talked about our cities, about how we trained for the Camino, about food. I've seen them on the road and in albergues all the way back since Getaria.

It turns out that Xavier went to Santander and this kind of proves Johns' theory about him and his competitiveness. I asked Didier why and he raised his shoulders and said "to walk more". I'm quite surprised that he left Didier and Sophia behind, they seemed like a close team together. Maybe he thought that I would also be heading towards Santander. I thought about going the extra mile too in Guemes, my energy level was OK and there was still plenty of time left in the day but I was thirsty and the lack of the water on the road made me want to cling for a more safer place for the moment.

At the albergue I see many familiar faces, including the German girl. I take my first Camino shower. I put some of my clothes in the washing machine and pay 0.50E, Sophia and Didier also contributing. This place is quite nice and interesting, there are volunteers and there seems to be a community built around this place. I'm staying on a chair in the garden, bathing in the sun and listening to classical music thanks to the Korean guy. Arriving at this place I was in a strangely good mood. I asked the volunteer girl from Germany sitting at the reception desk if she is Abuelo Pedro – as a joke obviously. Didiers' email address looked made up, it was something like abcd1234...@hotmail.com. He says it's real.

Talking with Juliana I find out that John and her took a taxi from Laredo to Santona yesterday because they also missed the 14:30 PM boat.

Two French guys were helpful today with their

guides, I might have taken a wrong path. One of them wanted to drink from a source that didn't looked good for consumption. I asked a passing man about the water and he was like "I don't know".

I visited the little museum at the albergue. I have seen the Land Rover that has over 700000 kilometers done over Europe, Africa and South America. Ernesto Bustio is quite an explorer.

Had some sort of conference where the speaker was the warden from Santona's Alcatraz prison. The Italian guy, Tino, did a hilarious translation of the wardens' discourse from Spanish in English. His "help" was a French guy who didn't even knew much English. Very funny stuff.

At dinner I spoke with an old jovial man from Canada. He knows Spanish (lives in Oaxaca, Mexico), French (married a French Swiss woman), was a teacher in Switzerland, author of books. He tried to finish the Camino a few times before. We had an interesting conversation.

Day 10, 30 April, Santander

After the breakfast at the albergue, I slowly walked my way to the town of Somo. It was a lonely walk on a barely circulated highway. At some point, close to the beach and the cliffs in Somo, I am joined by the German girl from Islares, Juliana. We do some small talk. The wind is very strong and spoils the whole view and the walk across the beach. Sand is getting in my eyes and I'm struggling to maintain my stability and direction. I get frustrated because of the strong wind and decide to start running in order to escape the ordeal faster. So I run across the sand dunes and the beach for a good number of kilometers. I pass by most of the other pilgrims. The two French guys from yesterday are cheering me. I'm now feeling elated because of the beautiful scenery and the fact that I managed to get out of the strong wind. This also marks a premiere for me, my first run on the beach. I've seen people doing it before but I haven't done it myself. At some point I encounter the German mother and daughter team and the mother asks me "Why do you run?" "Why not? This is my first run on the beach" I answer.

I enter the little town of Somo and walk a few hundred meters to the embarcadero. I ask two passing men if they know where the boat to Santander comes but they say that they are not from around these parts. Arriving at a long bridge I notice a yellow sign pointing backwards. There weren't any people to ask around so I headed on the bridge to what seemed like a port a few kilometers ahead. The weather was starting to get dismal, a strong wind was blowing, there were dark, menacing clouds and bits of rain drops were pouring. My hat was almost blown off my head and I had problems maintaining my direction on the narrow pedestrian path on the bridge, the wind was pushing me towards the fast moving cars. I notice an incoming boat. I see a jogger running towards my direction and I ask him where the *barca* to Santander is. He says that the one that is entering the little harbor might be it, he is not sure and also tells me that maybe I should go to the bigger harbor that I have seen a few kilometers ahead. Given the worsening weather conditions and the fact that missing the boat would mean having to wait for the next one, exposed to the elements, I had to make a quick decision. My gut was telling me that going on that bridge was not a good decision (maybe that backward pointing yellow arrow helped in taking that decision too) and that the incoming boat was the one to Santander. I turn back and start running. On the pontoon there is now quite a flock of people waiting for the boat. I run until I hear the boats' horn and until I see the jogger starting to wave at me signaling to run quicker to the boat. He was talking to a man on the boat and he was probably telling him not to leave yet. Once I get into the boat I notice Didier, Sophia and the mother-daughter team inside. The mother said sorry for giving me bad directions, she said something about going on a bridge in our short discussion on the beach. The road by the boat was not bad but the experience was affected by the strong wind and the cold. The cost for the boat trip was 2.75 Euros.

In Santander I kept looking after a charger and on my second try at a Bazaar Canaris shop I manage to get a working one for 12 Euros. I notice the big beautiful blue eyes of the girl at the desk there.

I went to the tourism information center and there I got a map of Santander and the location of the albergue pinpointed on it. The albergue didn't seemed to be far from the tourism information center. The albergue was not that hard to find even though it's located in some sort of a back alley and it's a bit tricky to find.

The Santos Martires albergue doesn't open until 14:30 PM so I had about two hours to waste. I started looking for a supermercado. One man sees me wandering the streets and asks me what I'm looking for. "Supermercado?" "Go straight ahead until the end of the plaza and then turn right" he says. I follow his directions and find two Mercados, one next to the other and both with a little fruit market nearby. I stroll around the buildings and notice that they are actually fish and meat markets not actual supermarkets. I couldn't buy fish and raw meat to cook myself. At the little fruit market next to one of the bigger Mercados I buy three tangerines, "they have lots of water" says the lady at the counter, three bananas and two peaches for a total of 2.91 Euros. I wanted to leave the area but noticed in the meat Mercado that there are chorizo type of sausages in front of two stands. I go in to have a better look but end up staying a lot of time waiting in line at the two stands. I get annoyed and leave those stands. I finally buy from other stands in the Mercado a big, thick chorizo picante for 4.81 Euros, a queso and a dulce de membrillo (quince marmalade) who were packed together as an 2.90 Euros offer.

Back at the hostel. While waiting in line to pay I notice a guy with a small backpack, casually dressed. He pays, says that it's a donation and leaves. The woman at the desk asks "where are you going?". "I don't know where" he says. It seems that it was his first day on the Camino and I guess that he was looking for his first stamp. Staying at the hostel costs 10 Euros. The owner is an old lady that seems to have Parkinson because she is shaking all the time.

There are few people here at the hostel and unfamiliar faces. It's quite boring here. The place resembles a communist era apartment, old, in the WC room water is sipping everywhere, the toilet paper is moist. At least there is WIFI.

Yesterday and today I had to do some feet repairing, blisters are bugging me since day 7.

Day 11, 1 May, Santillana Del Mar

Started the day at about 7 AM. It took me about one hour – including a frugal breakfast – to pack and leave. While crossing Santander I had the impression that the whole city is nothing but a mall with first floor shops paving all the way out of it. There are very few people at this early hour and it's also Sunday, I think. The road was pretty much in a straight line for the first kilometers out of Santander. Boring road, walking only on paved streets and my feet are troubling me. As of this moment I can only limp because of my blisters; it seems that from the road to Islares to here things are getting worse for my feet.

I see a nice view of the snow capped mountains, Picos de Europa I guess, at some point and even a rainbow rising from the foothills of the mountains. I stop a bit to enjoy the sight and to take a few pictures. From Bezana onwards I was on the lookout for a train to take since I heard from the peregrinos and the warden in Guemes that you have to take the train in Boo in order to avoid crossing on foot a bridge that is circulated only by trains. I was imagining that the bridge is spectacular, long and over two opposing cliffs over a deep gorge; it proved to be completely different in reality, it's short and over a small river.

In Boo I manage to locate the train station. Seeing the schedule I notice that I can take the train all the way to Requejado. The train would be in station at about 11:32 AM and arrive in Requejado ten minutes later. While sitting on a bench and waiting I notice a guy with glasses carrying some kind of book about trains. I couldn't have a lunch there on the bench since it meant taking a lot of stuff out of the backpack and there wasn't that much time left until the train arrived anyway. So, in order to kill some time I decided to start a conversation with the young man. He was wearing earphones and listening to something – just like me (I listened to an audio book on the road to take my mind off my hurting feet). I asked him if he is learning about trains. Turns out that he speaks a good English and is studying to become a train conductor. He showed me the contents of the book: train mechanics, electrical circuits, train devices, diesel trains...he had to learn all of this in a year. The book was nicely illustrated. Nice kid, his cheap shoes were a bit worn off and his conductor like pants were a bit splattered with mud. We talked about the fact that I want to get to Requejada, I said that I will do the Camino Lebaniego in the mountains, he asked me where I am from and the region, we also talked about the weather in Spain and the fact that in the North it's colder than the center and South of Spain, he said that it's between 25-26 degrees Celsius in the North in the summer and rainy in autumn and winter. He asked what regions in Romania I would recommend him. I said that in the South there is the Black Sea, not far from Bucharest...it actually depends on what do you want to see, there is also the Danube Delta which is an unique ecosystem in Europe and there are also the Carpathian Mountains in the center of the country with wild fauna like bears and wolves. He asked me how is Romania, I told him that compared with what I have seen so far in Spain it's some years behind Spain, there are worse roads, infrastructure, you should visit Romania if you want to go back in time and see wilderness and old traditions. Told me that the prices in Santillana Del Mar are high and in these kind of tourism based cities the prices are different for the locals and the foreigners. Told me that a bottle of water is 1.50 Euros in San Sebastian, 1 Euro in Cantabria and in Galicia 0.70 Euros, that Basque country is expensive. Told me that a train conductor has to call the police if he sees someone crossing a bridge like the one in Boo, the fine being a few hundred euros. Told me if there is no controller in the train then the ride is free, otherwise it would cost about 2 Euros to Requejada. He said that I should relax, walk slowly and enjoy the surroundings. He left the train one station before Requejada. We parted ways, shook hands and said to him that he will make a great conductor.

I eventually land in Baredo because I push the wrong button and the train door doesn't open so I am taken another station further. There I wandered around the station waiting for a train to take me back to Requejada when I suddenly notice the mother-daughter team on the bridge above the station. I asked what are they doing up there on the bridge and it seems from their answer that they took a shortcut and that Santillana Del Mar is now only about eight kilometers away not nine as my sheets were indicating. It turns out that getting one station further to Baredo was a good thing after all. I say "Cool!" and start crossing and jumping over the train tracks carefully since I didn't want any fine or to get injured, and to work my way up the stairs that lead to the bridge and a main highway. The yellow arrows are around again so I begin to follow them. Not long after, I see a big traffic sign, there are only five kilometers more to Santillana. "This is getting better and better!" I thought, being elated after the lucky turn of the events, my conversation with the future train conductor and the fact that I didn't had to pay for the train ticket. Well, the truth is that there were only five kilometers to Santillana by following the main highway, on the Camino however, things are different and taking the official route would most certainly mean taking detours from the highway which would amount to a longer distance.

After passing by an industrial zone, crossing a bridge and following the main highway I notice on a building written in large letters: Centro Comercial. Passing by the building I see that it has supplies and buying something to write on was on my shopping list so I end up getting inside the Centro Comercial. There I spend 5.40 Euros on: 1 Euro on Onduladas chips with sabor chamon – ate the bag at the nearby bus station while sitting on a bench in the shade, 1.80 Euro on 1l of Mosto Greip – concentrated grape juice, it's quite good and I love this thing, 1 Euro on a 1l box of El Conquistador Don Rodrigo red wine – I thought that I will need a tranquilizer later in the day after so much painful walking, 0.70 Euros on a long bread and 0.90 Euros on a new notebook. I tried paying with all the coins that I had on me, their weight is not negligible and it's already adding up to a heavy backpack, but their value amounted to only about 5.20 Euros. All those coins feel heavy in my pocket. While eating my chips and drinking the grape juice in the bus station I notice two peregrinos that I haven't seen before. I continue slowly and painfully on the road towards Santillana Del Mar. The future train conductor said that it has no actual connection to the sea. I jokingly said that it might have in the future (given the global warming and the melting of the polar ice caps). I stopped to take a break a few hundred meters from the entry to Santillana but not knowing it since I haven't seen any sign. A guy from Holland that I knew from the albergue in Santander was passing by and I asked him if he knew how much more is it to Santillana. He took out his guide book and told me that Santillana is less than one kilometer far. He went away. "See you at the albergue!"

While entering Santillana I notice a building that seemed to be a big castle. The stony streets are really hurting my feet with their pointy and irregular shaped stones . I feel each and every stone I'm stepping on. Santillana Del Mar has a medieval air to it, there are a lot of tourist strolling the streets, most of them seem to be Spanish, there are reconstructed old buildings but it all seems fake to me – there are shops, bars, hotels at every floor of every building just like in Santander. It seems to be a tourist trap so I'm eager to get off the stone streets and find somewhere to stay as soon as possible. I realize that there is actually not much to visit and following the yellow arrows I end up at some kind of complex which has bungalows, a restaurant, a cafeteria, a 'supermercado', a tennis court, a swimming pool and a place for caravans. The reception opened at 3:00 PM and the cost was 10 Euros. Sitting at the 'albergue', bungalow actually, was a bit lonely since it seemed that I was the only one staying there. I learn afterwards that somewhere in the plaza of Santilla there is an albergue, maybe an actual albergue, that costs only 6 Euros so I'm guessing that the others went there. At some point an Italian woman comes in my bungalow, does some unpacking, does some clicking at a computer or tablet (there was WIFI only at the restaurant) goes out and comes back for two times and then the third time leaves for good. A few minutes later the receptionist comes in, he checks the rooms, he smells, looking for god know what. I ask him what is he looking for, he says that the lady left, I say yes, I know that but I don't know why...we were both kind of puzzled. The receptionist says "I'm sorry" and leaves. The truth is that it gets quite lonely here without other peregrinos and I'm also missing the 'gang' that I met in the early days on the Camino.

Day 12, 2 May, San Vincente De La Barquera

Start of a new notebook. Start of a new day. First half of the day was quite amazing, I thought that today it would be 36 kilometers of agonizing walk on highways, paved roads and such, through the kingdom of boredom. Well, I did walk on highways, paved roads and other man-made structures that can be classified as roads but the scenery that I encountered today was well worth it. Agricultural fields and pastures with still sitting horses and slow moving cows, bulls and even several llamas. A few kilometers after Santillana the surroundings were dominated by an amazing church, made of stone and flanked by a palm tree. I took some pics to immortalize the great scenery. To the left there were the snow capped mountains, to the right there was the blue ocean. The village of Quesada has nice old looking buildings. It was hard not to keep starring at the mountains as they dominated much of today's landscape. I encountered old colonial looking buildings and churches. I read their descriptions in Spanish and it was an interesting experience. You could somehow feel the spirit of the conquistadors and the colonies that were once dominated by such buildings. Such places are veritable time machines.

Lots of springs and rivers originating in the mountains cross the land so getting water wasn't a problem at all.

I started my morning being quite relaxed, put my phone to charge and ate a frugal breakfast. Left at about 8:30 AM after checking the two rooms of the bungalow many times so I don't leave something important like a cable behind like I did in Portugalete. I had no idea where I'd be staying or how many kilometers I'd be doing today, it all depended on how my feet felt.

At some point I entered a lush green valley with agricultural fields, red clay soil and with a view of the mountains in their full splendor. It was quite a lonely road today, I resumed listening to my audiobook and walked slowly.

In a village close to the coast I get passed by a smoking woman; throughout the day we would pass by each other multiple times. She has a nonchalant behavior, walks slowly or quickly, smiles all the time, listens on her earphones, takes pics, speaks in Spanish with the locals and salutes fellow pilgrims. I've last seen her in Camillares, she was asking some locals about something in Spanish. In Camillares I've also seen Juliana ahead of me, I slowly followed her for a short while and then noticed her going to the left at some kind of Pessoa cubicle, maybe some kind of public toilet I don't know exactly what it is. I pass her but soon after she comes from behind and says something in German. She repeats her German twice and then I say "What?" She says "Sorry, I've been speaking German all day long with other pilgrims". Says "I'm going to get some postcards" and "see you tonight at the albergue". I ask: "Where are you heading to?" she: "San Verginia..." me: "San Vincente of something...?" "yes" me: "OK..." She seemed quite confused and tired.

Camillares has nice buildings and streets and a huge Jesuit college building dominating a hill, it looks imposing and awesome, but there I also find first floor shops, commercialism and a lot of what seems to be weekend Spanish tourists. After Camillares there are another nine kilometers to go. A last effort for the day. I notice a bridge over the river Ria...something with clear blue waters. Not long after I notice another river, Ria Capitan, with some kind of a mangroves thing going on a superb dune-like white beach. I notice the kite of a wind buggy surfer and three – kids maybe – playing ball on the beach.

I notice another pilgrim taking pics with what looked like some professional equipment. I begin to follow him. After a bridge he goes to the left following the main highway but I notice that the yellow arrow is pointing to the right to a forested coast. I say to myself that it's time for a shortcut, on the highway there are six kilometers to San Vincente, god knows how many on the detour. Following the highway I go up a hill and my feet and back (and stomach) are beginning to resign from the long march. Today I took very short breaks. At some point I see a dog trying to get under a fence and get out to "meet" me, it's a big white dog. He realizes that he can't crawl under the gap in the fence and goes to the main gate. It's clear that he was aiming for me. I cross to the other side after staying still for a short while and thinking about what to do if he manages to crawl out.

At an intersection I see the guy that I'm following going on some country road. I notice that the yellow arrows started to pop out again. I started to follow them again somewhere near a Taberna Valles sign. Surveying the surroundings I realize that following the yellow signs all the way would have resulted in a few kilometers more of walking. I slowly advance to San Vincente walking on dirt roads, roads paved with little white stones when I come upon a view that presents a little Venice looking kind of city. Mesmerizing. A sandy estuary with white boats. A big bridge for the highway. Another bridge that seems to be built from stone. A fortress on a hill. The mountains and something that looks like a swamp to the left.

I take pics, walk slowly and at the entrance of the city I catch up with the pilgrim. He is staring at his map on the phone. I ask "Do you know where is the albergue?" He shows me his phone and says "we are here and the albergue is here" pointing to the map, "calle Alto must be somewhere up the hill". We walk through the city when I suddenly notice a cafeteria and say that I'm going to check it out. There I buy a long bread for 0.88 Euros. At a another shop nearby I buy a chorizo for 5.9 Euros and a wine for 2.5 Euros. I wander the streets trying to find the albergue. I ask a car mechanic where is the albergue and he says that it's straight ahead and then take a turn to the left near the church. I eventually get to the Galleon albergue which has a big galleon sign on it. Max is a German guy in his early twenties who is volunteering there. He initially thinks that I'm German too. I unpack and take my newly acquired food out, sit on a chair in the warm sunlight (it's cold staying in the shade because of the breeze) for a feasting. People are arriving at the albergue. Some young guys traveling together and that I haven't seen before on the Camino (they are from Scotland, Germany, Ireland Barcelona) come to the albergue and then Juliana and Tino the Italian also arrive. The Austrian guy was already there when I got. Staying at the albergue costs 10 Euro, breakfast is included. A dog called Missy stands by me anxiously waiting for me to throw bits of chorizo that I can't chew. She ends up having a nice meal but later on she barks at me without any provocation. She shows no appreciation. I chat with Juliana and Tino and tell them that I'm not sure what to do next. I want to head toward the beautiful mountains and do the Camino Lebaniego. I eventually set on going on the Camino Lebaniego, it's a sad decision because that means going away from the Getaria gang and from Juliana. I have an interesting conversation with Max.

Day 13, 3 May, La Fuente

Today started with me going to the bathroom in the early morning. I see that Tino is also up. When I go back to my bunk bed he comes up to me with a blue jacket and gives it to me. Yesterday I was talking to him and telling that I decided to go in the mountains but I'm not really that prepared, I don't have warm clothes, it's cold here on the coast, I imagine that in the snow covered mountains it's even colder. He thought about it and decided to give me his good quality warm rainproof jacket. I was quite impressed by his gesture, said thank you and shook his hand. After breakfast I went to thank him again and hugged him. This nice gesture and the conversations that I had the night before will pre‹ my mind for the days to come. I got quite emotio The first kilometers of today's journey weren't anything spectacular, I walked on paved roads and highways following the red cross signs now.

Somewhere around Estrada I didn't continued to go straight on but continued to follow the main highway instead. The Camino Lebaniego is not that well marked. After about one kilometer I realized that I was off the Camino for sure since I haven't seen any sign. I had a road going to Portillo to the left and one going to Abanillas to the right. I;m reminded of the fact that I have a map with the Camino Lebaniego so I check it out and discover that this might actually be a shortcut by following the road to Abanillas and then continuing on the CA-181 road.

In Abanillas I have a great view of the mountains. The peaks didn't seemed that high now. On the way unchained dogs barked at me so I had to get a big walking stick that doubled as a defense stick. These mountain dogs can be quite big...and unchained. At some point the road seemed to take me to Pesues which was in the opposite direction of where I wanted to get to according to my map. I tried to remember if maybe I've missed something but couldn't come up with nothing. I didn't wanted to go back for some kilometers and try to find the Camino path so I decided to go towards Pesues then...at least I knew that heading that way I would eventually get back on the Camino Del Norte which is better then heading nowhere. Turns out that I actually got to on the CA-181 highway and after a short while the road forks again and this time the CA-181 takes a good turn towards the mountains leaving Pesues in the opposite direction. I followed it until Cades and crossed the bridge over the river Nansa. From Cades I followed the CA-856 road. Not much to say about Cades, it's a small village, the restaurant-bar is closed. I was already on the road for a while now and I was looking for food and water. The road through the mountains was pretty much like walking through a desert. Some cars, some cyclists, lonely houses spread across the road, small villages consisting only in a few houses. In Cades and Sobrelapena I found nothing. The odds of finding food seemed dismal, I began questioning myself "what am I doing in this desolate place, without food, without water?" In the mountains it's actually hot today, the sky is clear, there are no clouds and I remain without water having to drink it all to quench my thirst.

Turns out that the Austrian from yesterday is also doing the Lebaniego. I find that the Austrian's name is Kajetan. We end up in the small village of La Fuente. He speaks with a local. Apparently, the hospitalero is not at the albergue, the villager calls him. The villager asked me if I know Castillian, I said that I know some poquito espanol. The old man told us about the wolves that are coming at night to prey on the animals that are grazing the pastures surrounding the village. He had a pair of binoculars and showed us the vultures that were circling high in the sky over something. "Maybe over another peregrino" I joke.

Michal greets us. (it's not a typo, this is his Polish name)

Michal is quite a character. He speaks a good Spanish and a good English, he doesn't hurry up and takes his time, his moves are slow and calculated, he is pedantic, constantly adjusts his back. He is Polish but lived in Spain for the past ten years, he was a receptionist in Mallorca, a dancer and entertainer, worked in a shop. He stares at you with a crazed look, laughs suddenly and loudly. He runs and does yoga, is a vegetarian.

Kajetan is a reconstructive plastic surgeon living in the UK.

The three of us (we were the only ones in the albergue) talked about various subjects. Michal did most of the talking. He talked about weed, about the Popes' twitter updates, his life, the Camino, about the food in the mountains, about languages – while we ate. He served us a big pot almost full to the top with a hot porridge-like mix of vegetables like lentils, carrots, marigold, rice and others. While me and Kajetan did the eating, he was busy talking and chopping orange peels into small bits. He talked about the life here at the albergue, the life here in this remote village in the mountains. He is stuck here since last August, hitchhikes 100 kilometers or more to cities like Santander in order to bring food (and beer) at the albergue. There are not many kitchen utensils at the albergue so we have to make use of a cup to scoop up the food into our bowls. The food is good and it's a lot of it!

The cost of staying is 11 Euros but it's well worth it, this place is like an oasis in the mountains. The albergue is big, nice, clean and warm, it's one of the best albergues that I've been in so far. However, there are not many people that are coming at the albergue, yesterday there were three people and the most were in August last year, sixty in total for the whole month. I took a shower and clipped my nails afterward. Drank three beers for the price of 1 Euro each. Today's journey was quite hard and I didn't imagined that at the end of the day I would be showering in a nice place and eating a good, plentiful meal. Kajetan plans to return this summer in late July/August and maybe volunteer for two weeks. He plans to bring kitchen utensils with him and to donate them.

Kajetan said at some point while we were waiting in La Fuente: "don't worry, the Camino will provide", our situation was uncertain but he was absolutely right.

Day 14, 4 May, Potes

I woke at 6:30 AM, after some villager started up his loud grass cutting machine (I don't believe it to be a coincidence, I guess that he is the alarm clock of the village) but choose to be a bit lazy and stay a little bit more in bed. Served a tasty breakfast consisting in some kind of light porridge made from cereals, sliced fruits like bananas and apples, nuts, tiny bits of orange peels, honey. I also had a few spoons of my own honey that I had been carrying all the way from the Zenarruza monastery and that I used to supplement my morning caloric intakes. I was preparing for an arduous day ahead.

The arduous part didn't took much to come since about 200 meters from the albergue we started climbing up and up a steep incline towards the village of Cicera. We progressed slowly on the mountain slope which was to the right and to the left there were fences, pastures and grazing cows. No vultures. The path takes us to a highway and we walk a short while on it but not long after, the red cross signs take us to mountain dirt roads. It felt so good to have softer ground under my feet again! I haven't felt soft road ground like this since Bilbao. The progress is a bit slower because of the rocky road but it's still better than a highway. We follow the bumpy road down to the village of Cicera. Cicera seems to be larger than La Fuente and it even has a few modern houses and a bar! A truck carrying the weekly supplies arrives in the little plaza of the village starts honking. People are slowly starting to gather and K. takes his hat off and humbly asks for some bread. The driver says that he is not transporting bread and smiles. In Cicera we decide to follow the official Camino route marked by small white pillars with red crosses on them. So we continue going to the right even though a graffiti red arrow marked an alternative road to the left. We get out of the picturesque village of Cicera and start climbing, we couldn't see where the path would takes us but it seemed to go up the mountain and maybe over it and that didn't seemed to be a good prospect since it meant climbing up hundreds of meters of steep terrain. We follow the serpentine road, encounter deer scat and other pilgrims tracks. Arriving on top of the mountain, the view is well worth the effort, in front of us there are snow capped mountains and behind us is a beautiful valley with the village of Cicera and another small village in it. There are flowers, green grass, thorny brushes, mushrooms and dried, leafless trees. We start going downhill now and I think that the climbing is over. The feeling of relief is short and we are soon faced with going uphill again. We pass by a Abejas Trabajando sign on a fence surrounding several bee hives.

We see the Llebana valley before us and start going down on serpentines towards the village bellow. After the village, in distance, there seemed to be the highway that should take us directly to Potes. After this steep climb I was not eager to go to Cabanes and climb steep mountains again for the day. No more detours. The climb down seemed to never end as we do loops across the slopes of the valley. The path is heavily dotted with jagged rocks and small pebbles. In the village of Llebana I drink cold, clear, good and much needed water coming out from a pipe and straight from the mountain most probably. K. makes a stop in the old church and I take a wrong turn for a short while going on the road on the right side of the church. I had to track back to the church and follow the road made for cars. Not long after, I get to the main highway heading to Potes. I thought that K. got lost somewhere around the church but now I can see his red shirt in the distance.

On the highway, I see a team of three engineers, they were discussing some stuff, most probably about road maintenance. One of them looks at me, smiles and shows me the official Camino path and makes a gesture with his hand as if saying "over the mountain". I smile back and say "no...no". The mountain looks steep and damn tall. Not today, thank you kindly.

There are about eight kilometers more to Potes. "Not too bad" I think, maybe two hours more of walking, not more. I feel somehow energized by the thought and start walking briskly, my healed feet permitting me to do so. I leave behind my heavy walking stick and I soon catch up with Kajetan. The sun is up, it's the middle of the day, there are absolutely no clouds and it's hot. The temperature must be somewhere around 30 degrees Celsius I think (later on, in Potes, K. would say that he saw an electronic panel near a pharmacy showing that the temperature is 31 degrees Celsius). I try to keep my pace, keep soldering on and not to think about the heat and my back pain. To my right, down below, the river flows furiously; for a moment I felt like going down the steep terrain to put my aching feet in the river. I catch up with K., he says that his feet are tired and I leave him behind soon after. For the next few kilometers I keep looking back for him but I don't see him.

There are only three kilometers more to Potes. Buildings are starting to appear. There is a huge information center building about the Picos de Europa in Semana. I wanted to enter and visit it and ask some questions but I wanted my suffering to end even more.

At the entry of Potes I see a discount supermarket called Dia. The clerk was about to close shop between 14:30 PM and 16:00 PM (as almost all Spain does). There was only one other shopper there, an old lady staying at the cashier. Luckily, the cashier guy says to me that I can get in but I have to make it quick. I hurry up and run through the shop looking for stuff to buy. I was minding my own business when the guy shows up behind me as if he wanted to check up on me...I wasn't planning to steal anything. I spend 12 Euros on: Ruffles chips – 1 Euro, sliced Chorizo and Salchicon – 1.55 Euros, 500 gr. Of Cabra (goat) cheese – 4.95 Euros, 1.5l of Sangria Dia – 1.13 Euros, Mosto Greip – 1.64 Euros, 1.5l of Lemon Ice Tea – 0.72 Euros, long bread – 1.40 Euros.

On a bench nearby, I drink all the iced tea and eat half of the bag of chips and some chorizo with bread. I didn't hurried since it was hot outside and I was staying comfortably in shade on a bench and I was also thinking that the albergue might be closed at this hour – fact that would later prove to be correct.

I trek across the city, I could barely see any people on the streets, it's hot but I carry on. In my search for the albergue I ask people, go to the tourism information center, and even get to a private albergue and ask there were is the Albergue Municipal. I finally find it and wait because the doors were locked. The albergue is located somewhere down a little plaza with restaurants and bars and a big tower dominating the place. You see a sign for a bar called La Whis and nearby you have to go down some stairs in order to get to the albergue. K. comes and says that I have to get a key from the tourism information center which is now open. I go there, get a key and pay 5 Euros. I ask if I can stay one more day.

The albergue is quite big, with many dormitories,

60 places, it's nice and clean, there is a kitchen and even a big dinning room with lots of tables and chairs. There is only one other person staying, an older French woman. However, there is no WIFI so I have to go to the little park near the tourism center where there is a post with free WIFI. The Cantabrian government planted these posts and plans to add more all along the 72 kilometers of the Camino Lebaniego. I get an Internet connection and search information about the Picos de Europa mountains, hiking routes and how to get to Fuente De. There seems to be a bus to Fuente De but its schedule doesn't fit my needs.

Day 15, 5 May, Potes

Woke up a bit late, at 7:30 AM. The French woman left already. Finished what was left of yesterday's food.

Today's plan was to go to Santo Toribio monastery, get the Credential, see the Lignum Crucis, go to the tourism center at about 10:00 AM, ask there if they know about a solution to get to Fuente De and do a hike in the mountains, buy some food, do the hike and get back.

K. went ahead of me to Santo Toribio. Having to carry only my clothes, which is a novelty for me in the past two weeks, I started to go towards the monastery via the sign that I have seen yesterday. Turns out that the route is not marked that well so I had to backtrack and to ask someone where Santo Toribio is. He says that I have to go straight ahead and then take a turn to the left. Says that the hermita is on the hill. I look up and realize that I was going in the right direction but haven't noticed the hermita. I try to walk briskly. I get to the monastery quite fast (there are about three kilometers between Potes and Santo Toribio) only to see K. roaming around with his backpack on his back. Puzzled, I ask him why would he carry his backpack. He says that he has some food and water in it. We take some pics, inspect the grounds and then go further up the hill to the hermitas. Santo Toribio opens at 10:00 AM and there was still plenty more time left until then. I go up a rocky road and get to the Santa Catalina hermita. From the hilltop I look at the surrounding scenery and notice how small Potes looks from here. I notice the electric device that is used to automatically ring the hermita's bells. It seems that there is no need for Quasimodo nowadays to ring bells. The hermita is locked. I go back on the path only to see K. struggling up hill towards the Pedro hermita. A sign says that the Pedro hermita is at a distance of 666 meters. I decide to visit the Santa Cueva which is at a distance of 960 in other direction according to the same sign. Cueva (cave) sounds interesting and visiting a cave is one of my objectives in this trip. I climb up the hill again and get to a fork in the road. There are no signs, only stone cairns. I go further up the hill and after 2-3 more cairns I get to the "cave". Honestly, it was quite disappointing since the cave it's actually a man-made, stone made, very small room.

I decide to go back to the monastery and I even do a little jog down the hill. I stop at a Servicios water pipe to quench my thirst, I didn't carried any water with me and didn't expected to do so much climbing, plus, it was already starting to be a hot day. I get inside the little garden and the "museum". I get inside the church...it's dark, I remark the purple of the stained glass splayed on the ground, it was quiet, peaceful, cooler than outside. I roam around the empty church and notice the sarcophagus of Santo Toribio laid down in semi-obscurity, half-covered in light and half-covered in darkness it looked eerily alive with a great sense of peace emanating from the sculpted face. It reminded me the idea that death is nothing more than an eternal sleep. It reminded me of my own mortality. I look for the Lignum Crucis. On the other side of the church there is a small room, locked with iron gates, on it's glass walls there are symbols like Alpha and Omega, the beginning and the end. There is a wooden structure in the center of the room and I suspect that there might be the cross. I take a pic even though there is a sign indicating not to take pictures. I stay on a bench, in quite solitude. It felt quite good and I enjoyed the cooler temperature of the stone building. I observe the ceiling, the arcades. I would have stayed longer but I'm reminded that there is also a big hike to do for today.

I run pretty much all the way back to Potes and to the tourism center. I pay there another 5 Euros for the day and ask for a bus schedule. Taking a bus to Espinama at 14:30 PM didn't seemed like a viable option. From there to Fuente De are 3 kilometers (on the highway) and then what? I get to Fuente De, get in the cable car, enjoy the nice view, get back down and then walk back 22 kilometers?

I go to the Lupa supermarket that I have seen yesterday while going through the city. There I spend 19.82 Euros on: 1l of Tinto Verano Sangria – 1 Euro, 2 big breads, 500 gr. each – 1.40 Euros each, Sidra Camin Natural 70 cl. - 1.99 Euros, queso Alteza Provolone 200 gr., 2x1.99 Euros, chorizo Alteza Sarta Picante 280 gr., 3x1.99 Euros, freson bandeja (strawberries), 500 gr. - 0.99 Euros, naranjas, 4 kg – 2.99 Euros. I bought food for today and for the next two days.

On the road to Lupa I noticed the Rutas 4WD Picos Tour travel and adventure agency so I went in and looked around. A circuit of the Picos de Europa to the Garganta Del Cares done in a 4x4 car and a 12 kilometers long hike across the gorge costs 50 Euros. I took a leaflet.

I get back at the albergue, eat some of the food. I wasn't sure what to do next and K. told me that there is some kind of a castle around here somewhere so I decided to roam the city. I navigate through narrow streets and old looking buildings and took pics. I pass by a Mexican themed restaurant and I'm suddenly reminded of one of my bucket-list items: to drink a Jarritos! I enter full of high hopes and not much long after squinting inside I see them little bottles placed in the center of the bar, waiting for me. I hop on a chair with direct access to the bottles and start looking and comparing. There were five flavors to choose from. I ask the barman which is the mejor, he didn't knew what to say so I say "depende?" "si". I take the guava flavored one since it looks the most exotic. The taste is not bad, it was actually good as a matter of fact but I was disappointed by the fact that they are not that natural as I thought. A bottle of Jarritos contains agua and azucar mostly along with some flavors and acidifiants. Cost: 2.50 Euros a bottle.

I go to a religious themed museum that is located inside the tower about 20 meters away from the albergue. I wanted to visit it just to pass some time. Once inside I find out that it costs 3 Euros. I thought that it's free. The receptionist there said that it was free in 2011 (the sign advertising that it's free still remained posted) so I decided to skip it. I google Fuente De on Google images and realize that is not much of a big deal. I go back to the albergue and decide to abandon the whole Fuente De plan. K. is also back, says that the castle was too far to visit it. He said that at the monastery he saw the Lignum Crucis, that hoards of Spanish and Dutch picture taking tourists were there (I saw the tourist buses marked with E and NL coming up on my run down to Potes) and that he bought the credential from the monastery shop for 1 Euro. I asked him to show it to me so I know what I lost. Turns out that the credential is not that much of a deal, it's only a generic kind of diploma. However, I was a bit disappointed that I haven't at least seen the cross after doing the Camino Lebaniego on foot across a harsh mountainous landscape. It seems that they bother to open the gates to the Lignum Crucis only to hoards of tourists, screw the early, lonely pilgrim!

Some Spanish guys arrive, all of them quite old, except one of them that looks to be around 30 years old maybe. I stay in my bed thinking at various things. I can't stay for too long this way and I go back to the tourism office to pay 5 Euros for another day. I was pushing my luck. There, they say that normally they allow only a one night stay for pilgrims, that it's not a hotel, but I'm granted a permission to stay for one extra day after explaining that I intend to do a circuit to Garganta del Cares. I ask about the weather since there are dark clouds over the city now and the wind picked up. Rain and thunders tonight, rain tomorrow and a chance of thunders, rain for the next days. I take a little walk across the city hoping to visit the witch and witchcraft themed museum but it's closed. I see some new parts of the town and re-see others. I pass again by the Mexican restaurant but it's closed now. I would have drink another Jarritos just to pass some time and to quench my thirst of Jarritos for good.

I really like the old look of the buildings in Potes and the narrow streets made of stones, walking across them you are taking a trip back in time but it seems that it's only an illusion of old. The stone walls of the houses are only a facade, there is a modern brick wall behind them. The stone streets, which are not that great by the way, with stones extruding out of the pavement are also a modern effort made my the Cantabrian government between 2007-2010.

I get back at the albergue and review the pics and videos taken until now. I get melancholic, I am reminded that I have been through some amazing and incredible places and met interesting people along the way. It can get boring staying in a little place for too long. Outside is raining heavily now.

Day 16, 6 May, Potes

My Camino Lebaniego theoretically ended yesterday at the moment when I reached Santo Toribio monastery but for the sake of geography and the Camino's anatomy, Potes is located on the path of the Camino so I'm still on the Camino. Hopefully, this will change by tomorrow.

Today's plan was to go to Garganta's Del Cares on a 9:00-17:30 (approximately) day trip. I arrive early at the travel agency at about 8:22 AM only to find out that the 4x4 car was already booked. The owner said that it was booked by two guys from Switzerland that are staying at the camping site outside Potes which is near the S.T monastery. I should have booked the car since yesterday. This turn of events really put a wrench on today's plan. What was I supposed to do for the rest of the day here? I get back at the albergue and start working at a plan of attack to get me out of here.

K. is going back home and I have to part ways with him again. That's too bad because he is a funny and an all-around great guy. He is going to Santander back by bus; he has to go back to work but he might return this summer to do some more of the Camino. He says that it's a small world and that we will keep in touch by email. It's quite lonely to be in this big albergue all by myself.

I scramble to come up with a plan for the next

days and weeks ahead. The plan would be to continue via the Vadiniense route southward through the mountains and end up on the Camino Frances somewhere near Leon. The problem is that I have no accurate map of the Vadiniense route. I move through the dormitories trying to get a good Internet connection but the connectivity is weak, the speed is low and it keeps getting interrupted. I google, I wait, I have to connect again to the Camino En Red (the initiative of the Cantabrian government to plant solar powered WIFI pillars all the way of the Camino Lebaniego).

I eventually find something on a website, a guide, but I have to create an account, of course, in order to download it. I then find a map on Wikiloc but here I also have to create an account. I try to create an account a few times, username is taken, everything is going so slow...I try to log in, it doesn't work – email has to be activated, I enter my gmail account, access the email and click on the email verification link...nothing happens, I click again, and again nothing happens...I have to try and do a copy/paste of the damned link and finally succeed. I log in again, go to the map, try to download it...now I get several options, I go with using the Android one (which seemed like a good idea), it takes me to download the Wikiloc application, I try to download the app but it gets stuck at 3%...I try to connect to the WIFI again and somehow the download starts again and I succeed in downloading the app. Victory. When I install the app I notice in the installation manifest that the app requires Internet access permissions which might be a problem because I won't be having an Internet connection on the freaking road. I open the app. I have to enable GPS access. OK, I enable GPS access. I open the app again, now I need to log in with a username and a password. Fuuuck! I won't have Internet on the road so it means that the app won't work . I delete the app. I try to download the map in a GPX format this time. I finally download it. I open the map but I obviously need now a new specialized app that can handle the format. Time to google what kind of map do I need to install in order to be able to see the map. I click a promising link but the connection stalls...stalls and stalls some more. Fuuuck! I did all of this "progress" while my connection kept falling, when it worked the speed was slow and for some reason my phone's screen kept changing between the landscape and portrait screens like it was possessed.

The complete madness of technology. It should be fairly simple to get a map and to view it. Technology should simplify things, not complicate them.

They don't have maps at the tourist center, I asked before. Getting what I need from the Internet seems like the work of the mythical Sisyphus who was punished by the gods for his self-aggrandizing craftiness and deceitfulness by being forced to roll an immense boulder up a hill, only to watch it roll back down, repeating this action for eternity. Even if I will get a map I will he highly suspicious about the accuracy of it because of my bad experience with the Camino Lebaniego map. The highly inaccurate map that I currently have (from another Cantabrian tourism center) shows restaurants, shops, albergues, ATM's in what are in reality small villages that don't have anything in them. I know this as a fact since I passed through them and if it happens to be a small restaurant-bar there are good chances that it's closed. My map even shows that in Sobrelapena is a "cash machine". Buahahaha!

I can't make a plan for the next 200 kilometers of desolate mountainous terrain if I don't know where I can eat, drink or what path to take. I highly suspect that the ruta Vadiniense is very similar with the Camino Lebaniego. On a forum I read that there are albergues only in Potes, Cisterna and Gradefes on the route. I'm already in Potes and Cisterna and Gradefes are on the final stages of the route with an only 22.8 kilometers distance between them. My map shows "albergues" in Riano, Portilla de la Reina, Espinama in what are classified as highly touristic zones and I have my doubts about their existence. Most probably, there is only high priced accommodation in those places.

All in all, inaccurate information, incertitude, the difficulty of getting accurate maps and information make me unsure of the whole thing. I have a moment of clarity and I realize that I can just go back and continue the Camino Del Norte. After all, what's after ruta Vadiniense? It's the Camino Frances, much more popular and thus more populated and I'm not that much into walking along masses of people. I check one of the bus schedules that are posted at the front desk at the albergue's entrance. Salidas de Potes dirreccion Santander-Unquera 17.05 h. Not bad! I have plenty of time to rest and to eat some of my heavy rations of food. I'll just take the bus, arrive in Unquera, which is only one stage after San Vincente and check-in at the albergue.

I live for a short while with the impression that I will be in Unquera by tonight until I check my sheet of paper containing information about the Camino Del Norte with locations, distances between them, distance left until Santiago, the presence of albergues in the specified locations, otros alojamientos, camping sites, albergues solo verano, bars, tienda de alimentacion, farmacia, asistencia medica, cajeros automaticos, reparacion de bicicletas. Very useful little piece of sheet! The lady from the Santander albergue gave it to me. I check information for Unquera and I see that there is a small *a* instead of a big *A* meaning that the albergue is opened only in summer time. Damn. The next albergue is in Buelna, about 9 kilometers after Unquera but I realize that it's a tight squeeze. Recollecting from my experience up until now, most, if not in fact all of them albergues are opened until 20:00. There is a good chance that I might not make it there on time. I don't know when the bus gets in Unquera and I don't know how much time it will take for me to navigate myself out of Unquera and into the albergue in Buelna. Maybe it would be wise to leave it for tomorrow. I paid another 5 Euros for today's accommodation, I still have plenty of food to eat and a day off wouldn't be that bad after all.

Two Spanish guys come in to stay at the albergue. They camp in and after a while one of them comes and starts speaking in Spanish and saying stuff about ropas. I ask if he can speak English because I can't understand him. He calls his mate, Xavier, who speaks English. "He asked if he can use the washing machine", "of course" I say. He said that they came from Cicera after taking a bus there. They plan to do the Vadiniense route, the Camino Frances for a short distance and from somewhere near Leon they want to hop on the Primitivo. They don't have a plan about what to do from the Primitivo onwards, they will see about that. I feel the need to join the Spanish team in their adventure and I think about it for a while. There would be the language barrier, maybe they are faster than me – they look fit even though they are older. I remember one of them saying that he wants to arrive to Fuente De tomorrow and that there is no albergue there, they might share a room in a more expensive accommodation. Also...taking on the Primitivo to the north would mean going up to the Camino Del Norte again...so doing the Ruta Vadiniense, the Primitivo and the rest of the Camino Del Norte would extend my journey and mileage considerably. All of these contra-arguments made me reticent of joining them. The pro argument would be that the routes might take me through more wilder, beautiful scenery. And maybe less highways. From my experience with the Lebaniego, going through the wild and less popular route hasn't proved to be that satisfactory. Is this what I want? What do I want from the Camino anyway? Why am I doing the Camino? I don't have all the answers but at this point one thing is certain: I want to get to Santiago, I want to finish the Camino. This would complete my mission. I haven't achieved great things in life, I haven't finished many things...I should, at least, finish the Camino.

I go to the bus station to check the schedule. Tomorrow, Saturday, there is a bus to Unquera at 9:20. On the way back I buy a bottle of Monte Aragon Crianza wine. Cost: 1.79 Euros at the Lupa supermarket. Apparently, the wine is "fermentado en forma tradicional", it doesn't say on its label that it contains sulfites. "Color rubio intenso, adecuado para asados, caza y quesos currados o semicurados". Cheers! I really like the taste of it and its label colored in black, blue and white.

Three other Spanish people get in the albergue because the two Spanish guys didn't locked the door. It's late and the tourism office is closed. They look like hikers. One of them went into the city and came back at about 23:40. He tried the door, noticed that it's closed and then phoned his friend to let him in. His friend, not having any key, forced the door open. I get up, get my key and see what all the commotion is about. The door was forced pretty good so it wasn't easy to lock it again. The lock mechanism was a bit damaged. These people are crazy. The guy that forced the door looks dubious, he has a bandit kind of look on his face. I go to the kitchen to drink some water and there he is, the third Spanish guy who apparently is not traveling together with the two troublesome ones. He has a scared, maybe guilty look on his face. What kind of peregrinos are these? Coming in the albergue this late and staying up so late? From my experience up until now, the peregrinos are tired after a long day of walking on hills with their heavy backpacks, they go early to bed and get up early.

I'm writing these lines the next morning, it's past 8

AM now, I'm preparing to go to the bus station but the two troublesome Spanish guys are out and about. They left and told me that they are at the El Toro bar, I told them twice that I will be leaving at 9 AM. The third one is on the way to the Santo Toribio monastery, he said that afterwards he will hitchhike to Leon where he has a friend. Going into the kitchen and opening the fridge I find out that my last chorizo is missing. I should be more careful about leaving my stuff in shared spaces. I'm waiting and waiting but these people are not back yet. It's 9 AM now and I have to go to the bus station. I'm the only person in the albergue that has a key and I feel that it's my responsibility to not leave the doors unlocked. "I'm going to lock these people out or in if need be, I'm responsible to close and to deliver the keys, I don't have time to wait for these people" I say to myself.

I couldn't go to sleep last night, sat and thought at various things like the newcomers, the door. I opened the windows just like K. used to do so that I can have some ambient noise of the flowing water of the river below and the music of a bar nearby to put me to sleep. Even with the new changes I still couldn't sleep.

Day 17, 7 May, Buelna

I got out of the albergue at 9 AM after leaving a "Go to the tourism center" message on the door and locking the three of them out. I get on time at the bus station at 9:10 and stroll around anxiously waiting and wanting to get out of Potes as soon as possible. It's now past 9:20 AM and I start wondering what is going on since there isn't any movement around the station. I go to the cafe-bar near the station and a man there says that the bus to Unquera is at half past six PM. I can't believe what I'm hearing. Incredulously, I bring him to the bus schedule. Turns out that I have been reading the bus schedule wrong and that the next bus to Unquera is at 17:45 PM. The previous bus left this morning at 8:30 AM. Damn! That's eight more hours left to stay here in Potes! So what can I do for eight hours? I can't get back to the albergue, I just left the key under a rock near the door of the tourism center as I was instructed to do and there are also the three guys that I don't want to deal with anymore.

There is not much to do in Potes. I wait on a bench outside the cafe-bar. In front of me there are campesinos with sticks, herding cows and bulls, trucks that are bringing more cows to be put behind square fences. There is also hay. The sound of the bells that the cows are wearing around their necks is incredibly loud, a cacophony of sounds that makes me want to go to a more quieter place. I'm already stressed out and the noise from a heard of cows is not helping. However, I sit to observe what seemed like a cow trade show. I get fed up after a while and try to come up with things to do in Potes. The Brujeria museum seemed interesting so I gave it one more go but no, it's closed, for ever it seems. I'm not sure what is the connection between Potes and witches but I can see why some people would go crazy and start accusing other people of witchcraft. Potes makes you do it.

I follow the full length of the river promenade. I sit on a bench, eat a bit and observe two fat, lazy ducks. They are so lazy and get so much junk food from tourists that they are not even bothering to go after food that is further than their necks can stretch to. I go at the Mexican restaurant for another Jarritos. I hoped to get the Tamarind flavored one but it was already drank so I had to get a Mango flavored one. I also wanted to get rid of all the small change that I accumulated and carried around because it really started to have a considerable weight now. I get a big 300 grams bag of Lays for 1.85 Euros and paid in coins for it of course. I go back at the bus station, there are campesinos, breeders, dressed in jeans, shirts and boots, limping around with their sticks and bowed legs. They look like a pack of cowboys. It seems that now some cows have ribbons on their heads. They don't seem to notice the fact that they won something. The cows are only interested in eating hay and bellowing from time to time. I do a bit of slow walking across the streets in order to pass the time.

It's 17:20 PM now and I'm staying on a bench in a small park near the bus station which has a generic equestrian statue dedicated to the rural medic. I was counting down the minutes left until 17:45 when the two Spanish guys appear out of nowhere. Damn. They arrive and stay on a bench in front of me. We salute each other. Turns out that they are also waiting for the bus and heading to Unquera. No way! No way that they are going to Unquera! I don't want to see them in other albergues or on the Camino. The bus finally arrives and

I find out that they are actually going to Santander which is a huge relief for me. Things are finally starting to improve. Good riddance Potes, good riddance dubious Spanish guys.

The bus costs 2.9 Euros for a journey of about 31 kilometers to Unquera. The ride was spectacular and most of the thirty something kilometers were through a canyon formed by the Deva river. Very spectacular. Karst formations, caves, tall walls of rocks to the left and to the right. Tight curbs and a perilous drop down to the river make the trip quite exciting. Close to Unquera the rivers' color turns to an astonishing mix of green and blue. There is mist on the surrounding heights and dark clouds above.

The plan was to find an albergue in Unquera but nobody seemed to know if there is one. So I have to make a change of plan and head to Buelna by 20:00 PM. I would have staid in Unquera and close to the beautiful Deva river but with the fact that the albergue might not exist or be closed in mind I had to make a quick decision.

I quickly walk across the town and quickly climb up the steep hill outside of Unquera. "Are you kidding me? How am I going to do the 9 kilometers to Buelna on time on this kind of terrain?" I thought. I kept a quick pace until I went into a full run, helped by the fact that I was quite rested and my feet healed after not doing physical demanding activities in Potes. I run for a while, make a soul crushing u-turn, go across a bridge, across a rocky road. There are about five kilometers more to Buelna and it's 19:30 PM. There is no way that I can make the five kilometers in half an hour. I give up running and winded by the heavy backpack say to myself "que sera sera, whatever will be, will be, if there is nothing opened at that hour I still have a headlamp and I'm prepared to walk all night, if need be, all the way to Ribadesella". I keep walking fast, go through some more rocky roads, a dark forested area and get back on an old acquaintance of mine, the N-634 highway. To my right there is the dark ocean, to my left there is a wall of hills, above me there are dark clouds.

I get to the albergue somewhere after 8:30 PM. I approach the building cautiously...there are no lights, no movement around it and inside. It seems to be closed...wait! There is some light and there is someone in what seems to be a dinning room. I get closer and notice the schedule. The place is open until 22:30 PM. Yes! I made it!

The cost at the Santa Maria albergue is 10 Euros. I also ordered cena, dinner, at a price of 6 Euros. I am served two dishes, one consisting of a big plate of salad made from eggs, corn, olives, carrots and other vegetables and the other dish consisting in a plate full of pasta. I have a pleasant conversation with two other peregrinos dinning at a table next to me, a girl from Australia and a girl from Italy. Their happy nature, warm and friendly attitude make my day.

The wooden floor is heated. The room is warm, most probably there is some fireplace somewhere under the dormitory in which I'm staying but there is smoke and the smell of smoke that is seeping inside the room. The air is quite foul to breath and I think that there might be a probability that I might end up dying from monoxide carbon poisoning. I discover in the morning that I'm still alive and that I have a big swelling. I catch and kill a big flea later on and he seems to be the source of my big swelling. This or food poisoning. It's probable that I might have gotten flies while waiting on the bench at the bus station, there were big, shepherd dogs roaming around and campesions sitting at the tables outside. At some point, while sitting on the bench, a little flea landed on my forehead.

Day 18, 8 May, Pineres de Pria

Today was a long day, I walked since about 7:30 AM to 19:30 PM for a distance of 30 kilometers. The last kilometers were particularly tough, my feet started aching again and the roads were full of small rocks.

The objective of today was to get to the albergue in Pineres de Pria. I got there but it was full so the owner volunteered to give me a ride one kilometer up the hill to another location. I was disappointed by the fact that after a long and tough march I couldn't achieve my objective but it turns out that the staying at the albergue on the hill was a great experience.

All this time on the Camino I've been seeing and taking pictures of old houses made of stone and wood, well it seems that now I'm living in one and I got to see how it looks from the inside. Stone walls, the kitchen window is made from wood, no glass, the door entrance is made from bricks, stone stairway, wood beams, basic kitchen, basic bunk beds with an old look to them, straw filled pillows. The albergue is basic but you get an authentic experience.

The owner is an old man, he is very servile, he carried my backpack even though I objected. There is only one other peregrino here, a Spanish guy. From the owner's conversation with the other albergue owner that brought me here I understood that not a lot of people get here. The albergue doesn't even appear in my sheet which serves me as a guide. The albergue in Pineres de Pria gets all the attention and also the peregrinos. I would say that this albergue is a hidden gem in the rough for all those interested in a more authentic experience, quite similar to what the peregrinos from some centuries ago would have experienced.

I ask if there is some place where I can eat or buy food but the restaurant is one kilometer down the hill and considering that I arrived limping at the albergue in Pineres it's a no go for me. Also, the owner said that it's closing soon. He offered me an orange and an apple so I took the orange and left the apple, I don't have anything against apples, as a matter of fact I eat lots of them, but I didn't wanted to seem greedy. He also brought me two clementines and four apricots afterwards. Much appreciated! I had only a few rations left from a trip to a supermarket earlier in the day. There I bought a 1.5 l bottle of water for 0.35 Euros because I was quite thirsty, a medium sized bread for 0.80 Euros, sliced chorizo for 1 Euro, sliced queso for 1.60 Euros. Total: 3.75 Euros. I went with the principle that is better to travel lighter and not to carry with me a lot of food.

The albergue is donativo but you have to pay 5 Euros which is not much. So my costs for today are under 10 Euros which is not bad but the downside is that I'm quite hungry. On this Camino I have no idea how big is the next location, if it has supermercados (and even if it has, they might be closed). Today is Sunday, Domingo, so the supermarkets in Nueva were closed, there were only bars with people watching soccer in them that were available.

Here is quiet and peaceful, the albergue is very near a church and a cemetery – and probably that's why the owner smiled when I asked if there is any food in this direction and pointed on the other side of the hill and the cemetery that I didn't knew it was there. Not long ago I was living in a phonic hell with cows and bells. I got the authentic experience that I was looking for.

It was a cold night at the albergue since there is no heating, only cold rocks, I had two blankets on me but I was still cold.

At the beach that comes after Buelna I walked on gravel roads among vegetation of thorny bushes with yellow flowers and eucalyptus trees. There were bees around, doing their jobs and inspecting the yellow flowers. I got to the Bufoneria but didn't saw water coming, I only heard the howling of the wind. Soon after the beach I see a man nonchalantly caring his backpack on a contraption on wheels which is attached to his waist. "Genial!" would have said Xavier with a French accent.

Ate about a dozen of tasty and big raspberries when I walked through a field.

The road took me up on the sand dunes that overlook the town of Llanes. There I walked near the edge of a golf course, I saw people playing gold and I wanted to intrude and play golf – playing golf would have been a premiere for me. Maybe I should forget about getting to some location and instead get involved more, mingle a bit, do some stuff that I haven't done before. The Camino took me through the outskirts of Llanes so I didn't got to see more of the city. Outside of Llanes there was a sign indicating the fact that there are 29 kilometers more to Ribadesella - on the highway – which seemed doable. At some point I go for a while out of the Camino path in favor of some softer ground, I crossed a train track and managed to get back on the Camino without getting lost.

I got lost after Niembo because the route was not properly marked. I wasted maybe an hour backtracking and then backtracking again. An old lady saw me from the balcony of her house, shouted and made signs indicating the right direction. I went with her direction (for a third time), tracked back until I was about 100 meters after the sign that shows - Barru 2 km – and found that little pillar that shows the way of the Camino. It was masked by high and dense vegetation. I found a light stick nearby (that became my walking stick) and used it to clean (to beat) the vegetation into submission.

I also made a small cairn. I proceeded through a bit of a forested area on a gravel path and welcomed the shade because the morning clouds gave way in the afternoon for sunlight and high temperatures. I didn't welcomed the little rocks on the path that I had to constantly feel them under my feet. The road took me to the Antolin playa were I took off my shoes and put my feet in the cold water after having to tiptoe across jagged rocks and debris. After that, I walked in my Xero sandals for a little while but to no avail, my feet were still hurting.

In Guergu I notice, again, a type of a small wooden house on stilts. It seems to be specific to the Asturias region. Not long after the little house on stilts, there is a sign indicating that there are 3.5 kilometers more to Pineres de Pria and the albergue. It gave me hope, "3.5 kilometers is not much left, it's less than an hour of walking" I thought. Those few kilometers would prove to be more difficult that I thought.

Day 19, 9 May, La Isla

Woke up at 7:00 AM "helped" by the old man's heavily tossing of things around. Having nothing to eat I just had to pack my stuff and leave. So it was an early start for me. I walked through the morning cold and through quiet locations. Two bins had a Camino theme drawn on them with peregrinos. It's a cute gesture made by the local kids. The path takes me through train tracks and then a road close to the coast. On that road I feel soft ground under my feet and I can't believe it. I poke it with my walking stick again. Sand. Finally, there is something more decent to walk on even though rocks of various sizes are omnipresent. The road narrows into some kind of channel surrounded by dirt walls. After the walled section, green pastures and the occasional thorny bush are to be seen. I felt the effect of pour nourishment in the past two days. I was walking alone, just me and my thoughts.

Before walking the coastal road I went through Cuerres where there is a Peregrinos spring, Fuente De Los Peregrinos. Unfortunately, the water is not potable. In Cuerres I had reached a milestone: I've walked more than half of the Caminos' distance. The little sheet that I'm using now instead of a guide book shows 410.9 kilometers done until now and 406.1 kilometers more to go.

I walk for about two hours without encountering any pilgrim soul. Somewhere near an intersection and near a stadium I make a little stop. I get passed by two older Spanish guys. I've seen both of them the day before, one of them has an earring, an umbrella and wears running shoes, walks casually.

I follow the highway and in no time I am in Ribadesella. It didn't seemed like a long or a hard journey even though I am quite famished. I followed the arrows through narrow streets, walls with lots of potted flowers on them, white houses. Escalera de Colores is a stairway colored in various ways. There is also a quote that I'm not sure what it means. I get to the center and there I find a little supermarket which I have initially mistaken for a fruteria due to its outside fruit stands. There I spent 8.25 Euros on: platanos – 1.06 Euros, chorizo – 3.6 Euros, queso Fresca – 1.49 Euros, bread – 0.8 Euros, Aquarius – 1.3 Euros. I eat three of the bananas, drink some Aquarius (it's not that great, it's just water, sugar and a bunch of some artificial stuff). Iglesia de Santa Magdalena has a miniature look-alike of the Rio de Janeiro Jesus Christ statue on top. I go off the marked road and find a quiet place near a school overlooking the ocean. It's a perfect setting to have lunch, or breakfast since I've skipped it. I start strolling the streets and soon find myself on the promenade by the ocean. I go past various shops, find the adventure agency that was advertised in a flier that I found at the albergue in Buelna. The agency was closed with an iron grill. Not far, there is another adventure agency. The guy inside didn't spoke English so I explained to him in my Spanglish that I want to do the Garganta del Cares tour and what the price might be. I get a better price compared to the one from the agency in Potes, 35 Euros. "Not bad, in Potes it was 50 Euros" I think, but he says that his agency doesn't offer this service, opens an Internet browser, googles a name, opens a contact page and copies a telephone number on a piece of paper that he gives to me. I give him in return the flier from the competing agency that is closed. A telephone number? From another place? It seems by now that I shouldn't make plans based on fliers handed out by various agencies. I give up on any plans to get to the Garganta and back in the Picos de Europa mountains. There is no need to stay in Ribadesella anymore so I start following the arrows again. The tourism info center is closed on Mondays. I would have asked there for a map of the Asturias.

After Ribadesella, the marked path continues along the coast. Somewhere on the promenade I am reminded by the fact that I haven't went to the lavatory for the past two days. I sit on a bench trying to hold it in when suddenly the guy with the backpack on wheels passes by me. I get to the business of walking again and decide to do my dirty needs in a forested area close to San Pedru. There is no telling when the next albergue will come along the way so there is no need to prolong the holding and risk soiling myself. I pass by San Esteban where there is an albergue and where I was planning to stay. I follow a quite lengthy and peaceful gravel road until I see a sign saying La Vega. I realize that I passed San Esteban. Well then...the next place with an albergue is La Isla which is about 12 kilometers away. No problem, it's doable for today, there is plenty of time and sunlight left in the day.

I make my way down to La Vega and the playa. While walking through the quiet, deserted looking village I notice some nice drawings that seemed to be done by a contemporary Vermeer on the walls of a few buildings. At the playa I stop to eat a bit. There are surfers in the water and on the beach there is a guy with a tripod immortalizing their surfing. I see peregrinos slowly making their way up the steep looking hill behind me that overlooks the beach. My thought was that they must have taken another, harder, route since the sign seemed to point to another way. Wait...no, continuing by the beach there is a dead end, the big cliff that enters into the water is impassable. Damn. So up the steep hill I go. The uphill walk turns up to be a pleasant one, the hill offering shade, soft ground and luxuriant green vegetation. I make haste, emboldened by the better road conditions, cut straight through Brebes and end up on a sister highway of the old N-634 one, N-632. I wonder where did N-634 disappeared.

I get to a sign saying Concejo De Caravia. There, on an information panel, I get a glimpse of the path ahead. After a bit of uphill climbing and gravel roads I get to the beach again and start following the Camino Real along the coastline. Good road, nice view in front of me and to the right, no clouds, a bit hot. A cool looking stone road through high vegetation in a forested area made me think at the Pirates of the Caribbean movies. That area would make a nice décor for a pirate movie. Two old German women get on the wrong path and are trying to cross over some stone walls and wire fences. I've seen these kind of wire fences before and had the suspicion that they might be electrified. My suspicion is confirmed when I see at some point an electric cable connected to the fence and coming out from an underground tube. Fortunately, the German ladies successfully cross the obstacles and have a good laugh in the process. La Espasa beach is not far. Under a bridge on the road to La Isla, a hippie looking fellow is banging on a Caribbean drum. Pilgrims are starting to queue on the way to La Isla and the albergue. In La Isla I ask an old man where is the albergue. I get my answer and leave but I see the man with the backpack on wheels appearing from nowhere and asking the same man something. He goes in the opposite way of the albergue, towards the playa. I guess that he is staying at a hotel. I haven't seen him in albergues. He is nonchalant, dressed like he is going to the beach, likes to smoke giving the impression that he doesn't have any worry. He doesn't look like a peregrino, he seems to be a regular tourist. It's funny to see him on the Camino, the wheeled improvisation that he carries around seems to come out from his ass.

I get to the albergue that I thought is the albergue. An old lady, maybe in her eighties, or even more, comes. I have to fill a register with some information and to pay 5 Euros. The albergue is three minutes away, she says, just follow the signs. "You are the ninth pilgrim". I finally get there. Pilgrims are coming slowly but steady at the albergue and by night almost all the places are occupied. I read a fragment of a newspaper that is pined on a board. It's about a man who survived a shipwreck and walked more than 100000 kilometers around the world. I got to the albergue quite early, at about 16:30 PM. I wanted to search for a supermarket but gave up.

Day 20, 10 May, Villaviciosa

Woke up at 6:30 AM. The people start getting up one by one. Headlamps, zips, the dormitory door is opening and closing. Again, there is no breakfast for me so I just quickly pack my stuff (I learned to do it as part of the daily routine) – and leave. The guy that was saying yesterday that he is heading to Gijon seems to have left already. Maybe he left earlier than 6:30 AM, maybe at 4:00 AM, who knows, there are a lot of kilometers until Gijon.

I was quite happy to get away from the albergue crowd. I begin following the arrows but it seems that they are leading me backwards and at some point I also lose track of them so I head towards the center of the town and the main highway through which I came yesterday. The way to Colunga was pretty much a four kilometers long straight line. The road was pretty good and my feet were OK, the air was cold so I had a good pace partially due to being freshened up by the morning coolness.

At the entry of Colunga you are greeted with a sign saying "Museo del Jurasico de Asturias – 500 m". Sounded interesting but most probably it's not opened at this early hour. I notice colorful colonial style mansions on the sides of the road as you enter into Colunga. An old church dominates the center of the town. Nearby, a dilapidated old building with "Vende" signs plastered on it. A sign shows that the Jurassic Museum is to the right, the arrows and the highway continue straightforward so I just keep following them. Most shops are closed throughout the small city at this hour, only the Tobacco shop and some bar-cafeterias are open.

I get to the margin of the city being led by the arrows through narrow streets and soon I find myself on the N-632 highway again. There are 18 kilometers to Villaviciosa, 47 kilometers to Gijon. Why is Gijon farther away by taking the highway than following the Camino? I'm not sure. I'm not following the Camino anymore and soon after taking the N-632 I realize that there is no turning back. The road goes through sparsely populated places with no chances of encountering a supermarket, there is the same vegetation, green bushes, weeds, there is grass to my right and to my left, in distance, there is a chain of rocky mountainous formations that give way to smaller hills covered with a dense eucalyptus forest. After leaving Colunga the first settlement that I encounter is a place where people like sales so much that they named their small settlement after them: Sales. After Sales I encounter a little row of small, glued one to the other old houses. They are colorful and they display pots of flowers outside their walls. I notice yet another "There are deers ahead – for the next 1.5 kilometers" sign. I've seen lots of these signs until now but I have yet to see a deer. It seems that there are actually more signs than deers. In Chisquillo I notice a group of banana (here called platanes) trees. Unfortunately there are no bananas in them, there are no bananas today. This reminds me of the old "Yes! We have no bananas" song. At this point anything helps, even humming an old song, to keep my mind occupied and to forget the fact that I'm walking on a highway with monotonous scenery and there are still plenty of kilometers left to do on an empty stomach.

I get to a big, round intersection. To the right there a few kilometers to Llera. Even though the hike on the highway proved to be monotonous until now I made some quick progress so I thought that I might even get to Gijon today. Thus, I didn't bothered going left to Llera and try to find the Camino route. The little, less circulated N-632 transforms in a tumultuous river after it joins the A-8/E-70 which is a bigger highway forming a multiline highway. There are a lot of cars, plenty of trucks. Small stones, camouflaged by the asphalt. In front of me there is a team that seems to be tasked with the maintenance of the highway. They do some grass cutting. One of the grass cutters starts to yell at me and making signs that suggest the fact that I'm not allowed to walk across this highway, he also makes some ticket writing signs. "I don't want to get a fine" I think. A supervisor comes and tells me what I understood already, "red...N-632, over" and makes a hand gesture pointing across the highway to the left. I look and I think that I see another, smaller road on a small hill, camouflaged by vegetation. I quickly backtrack and somehow manage to get back on N-632 which seems to have changed places with the bigger highway which I now see it to my right.

This detour was quite disappointing. I walked slowly up the hill. I get to Alto de Buenos Aires, a name that I have seen on a map in Colunga. Seeing the name I thought that it sounded cool and that I'd like to get there. Unfortunately, as could be seen from that map publicly posted somewhere in the center of Colunga, the Camino doesn't go through Alto de Buenos Aires. Well, by not going on the Camino my wish is now granted so I find myself in Alto de Buenos Aires some kilometers after Colunga. What is Alto de Buenos Aires like? It's about three houses big, joined together like Siamese twins, with one of them having written on its facade: Alto de Buenos Aires. That's it. From top of the hill I have an amazing view of the valley in front of me. A big, low, lush green valley, watered by what looked like a big river flowing into the ocean. The view made me feel bad that I haven't followed the Camino as it's most probable that it goes through the valley. I meet an old man who carries a backpack and walks with a stick coming from the opposite way of the road. He begins to talk to me. Says that there are about 10 kilometers more to Villaviciosa, that Gijon is over a mountain - this didn't sounded too good for a hungry traveler like me.

The highway continues through a canyon corridor-like geography. Soon after, N-632 changes places again with the big highway, goes over it and now I have the big highway to my left. There are a lot of trucks on the big highway. I notice that in distance, the big highway goes on a lot of bridges, one of them is quite long. A feat of engineering, no doubt. There are eight kilometers more to Villaviciosa. There is reddish soil on the side of the road. Close to Sebraya the road turns into a long, straight line. The sun is starting to burn hot. I begin to smell the salty air. Maybe that wasn't a river estuary that I saw, maybe it was a prolongation of the ocean, some kind of a golf. I make a try to get out of the highway but get to a dead end. I notice an old house built in 1919. And then another, even older looking building. "Se vende". I decide to take a one minute break on the side of the road, in shade, and drink my last drops of water. After I get going on the highway again I notice another peregrino coming from behind. It's the earring and umbrella caring Spanish guy. We salute each other, he asks me if I'm OK, I ask him if there are albergues in Villaviciosa. "Claro que si". He goes off at a quick pace, maybe heading to Gijon.

Another episode of walking on a straight, long line. This time I notice something that looks like a group of modern looking buildings. It has to be Villaviciosa (I wonder where this name comes from). A Camino de Santiago sign appears and the yellow arrows are starting to pop up again on the sides of the road. I'm at the outskirts of the city. There are nice looking villas on both sides of the street. I see a La Plaza, 400 m, "Que poco cuesta comer bien" sign. I sure do hope so! I get to a park where there is a sculpture of a hat and apples, I go a little further and observe on the right side of the street the La Plaza supermarket. I cross the street and head that way. I spend 9 Euros on: 4 chocolate doughnuts – 1.08 Euros, 2 breads 330 gr. Each – 0.59 Euros each, 2 Mortadela Siciliana with olives – 1.37 each, 2 sliced Gouda queso – 1.19 Euros each, 870 grams of bananas – 0.86 Euros, Sangria Tinto Verano Clasico – 0.85 Euros, Oreos – 0.98 Euros. Not bad, I have about two days worth of supplies for less than ten Euros! I go back to the park to eat some of my newly acquired food. I drink the Sangria and not even half of it (and a 4.7% alcohol content) is enough to make me quite dizzy and drunk since I haven't eaten in many hours. I start searching for an albergue. I see the Italian woman from Buelna hanging out with the other old Spanish guy. I get to the tourism center. There I find out that there is an albergue close by "but it's private" says the woman at the reception. I try to find it but fail so I have to come back at the tourism office and get a map and the location of the albergue circled on it. I somehow manage to find the albergue after wandering though the streets. It's vis-a-vis from the beautiful Ateneo building by which I passed before while searching for the tourism info office. The cost is 13 Euros. The room is very nice and clean. I like it. Only one another guy from Australia is here. My bed is close to an old looking window and I have a view of the Ateneo. I eat some of the food, rest a bit and then head back to La Plaza which turns out to be only about 100 meters away from the albergue. At the supermarket I hunt some liquidacion wine that I have seen on my first trip. I buy a Vega Cubillas awarded with Medalla de Oro, Concurso Mundial Bruselas. Tinta del Pais grapes. It costs three Euros even though I thought that it costs two (turns out that it was put by mistake in the box with two Euros items). I also buy a 2l bottle of Fanta Lemon, which tastes quite good, for 1 Euro. The wine is dry, tastes a bit moldy.

I send an email back home with a few pics that I took on the Camino. I read online a bit about the Camino Primitivo, it seems to be something that I would like to do.

Day 21, 11 May, Gijon

Got up a little latter than usual, packed and started following the arrows. At some point my Musto Greip bottle (now filled with Fanta Lemon) manages to fall off my backpack and to spew acidulated Fanta all over. It's cracked at the bottom and I have no option but to throw it ain the nearest bin. The path takes me through a walkway, maybe 1 kilometer long. I see people doing their morning walk. On the outskirts of Villaviciosa there are more fancy colonial style buildings – must be all those people who returned from the Americas with riches. A water source and a sign telling the weary peregrino to trust that the water is good to drink. I didn't have any bottle to fill or any cup to drink from.

The arrows soon split in two: to the left to Oviedo and the Primitivo, to the right the road goes to Gijon. I choose to go right with the devil I know. The road takes me through a green forested area. All the dew, the morning coolness, the intense green, the presence of water nearby, the canopy made for a pleasurable walk. My feet were OK. At the exit of the canopy, stagnant water on the road attracts swarms of little flies. I wonder why they prefer to sit down in the water rather than swarm around animals like they usually do. The scenery opens up and I'm now walking through fields. To my left, green rolling hills. I guess that the Primitivo is full of these kind of hills. The arrows take me across the highway making an u-turn. I start listening to Marc Aurelius's Meditations. The arrows stop pointing backwards, they point left towards the hill top, an action that I anticipated that will come sooner or later given the fact that there are hills all over the area. The climb is slow but luckily, I now have my mind occupied. I notice a building that looks like a castle with high walls in front of it. It looks cool. The path goes up and up with an occasional trek through lonely houses. I go a bit offroad through a hole in the green wall to take pictures of the valley below. I see another peregrino making his way up. A new one that I haven't seen before.

The climb gives way to a more horizontal walk now and the height offers a great view of the valley bellow and the mountainous chain in distance. I'm in awe and take some moments to enjoy the view. The height, the surroundings, the cool air give me the feeling of being on Mount Olympus along with the gods. The climb is not over yet and I can see now the Polish, I think, couple make good use of their gas stove. The road finally starts going downwards. I'm emboldened and begin to sing, even though risking to dry my mouth even more. On one side of the hill some deforestation is going on. I can now see Gijon and the sea in distance, behind a hill. The walk gets more easy when you sing. From time to time I see breathless cyclists going slowly up the hill. They don't seem impressed with my singing.

Some more deforestation is going on. I see eucalyptus trees being cut. It doesn't seems to be an illegal operation going on, there are Trabajando signs and all. The arrows point to the left and downwards to the village at the bottom of the valley. Crossing it, I get at some point at a restaurant-bar which is closed. It has selling machines with small bottles of water which cost 1 Euro. The machines look old, I won't risk 1 Euro. The old peregrino that I have seen earlier is having some lunch, nearby, a Spanish couple is sitting and having a chat. In the village, I notice some manufacturing places that produce huge barrels. Sidra barrels most probably.

Not far after there is a water source, built due to a foundation back in the '50, and I quench my thirst. I remember that I have Oreos. I haven't eaten yet because I didn't want to dehydrate myself even more. A new climb over a new hill begins.

At some point the road transforms in a spring, water is flowing down across the rocks, creating mud and giving me the impression that I'm now walking uphill a river. The canopy forms a tunnel at the end of the climb. Some hundreds of steps later I'm overlooking Gijon. It's quite a big city but in about one hour I should be at the albergue, methinks. I would later be proved wrong. So down the hill I go. The arrows take me through residential looking places. In a forested area I make a stop for a few minutes. One tick gets on my bag, another one on top of the pocket of my backpack. There are also other types of insects crawling on my stuff. I get up, walk a few meters, stop in the middle of the dusty road and check and double check, I shake and pat my stuff and clothes. Ticks and the nasty diseases that they spread is the last thing that I need right now. I make a mental note to never stop in such a place again. It makes sense to be so many ticks given all the dogs and animals around. I stop following the official path because it seems to be taking me to the right, far from the center of the city and to higher ground. I had enough climbing for the day. I now wander the streets blindly, get to a dead end at some factory, pass by a big hospital, pass by a big college. In a bus station I see a map of the city. On the map I notice that there is an albergue, located somewhere on Palacio San Andres de Cornellana. I try to memorize as much information as I can and I also take a photo of the map. For the next hours I wander across the city, passing by the Terrorism Victims monument, a millennial old olive tree, a strange sculpture, a stadium, a hippodrome. I ask people to give a general direction towards Palacio San Andres and I get "Muy legos, a l'oeste" type of responses. I get to a Lidl supermarket, the first Lidl I have seen so far in Spain, and buy a 1.5 liter acidulated water for about 0.25 Euros. My pocket has a hole now (all the movement and constant friction might have caused it) so after I pay at the counter the change goes right through the hole and inside my pants. Coins come rolling out the sleeve of my pants and some even end up in my shoe. I would later find a coin in my shoe while taking a break from walking, I thought that it's a small rock, no, it turns out that it's a five eurocents coin.

I stop at a bench nearby and eat staying in the relentless sun. I do some more walking and see a row of taxis. At this point I'm quite defeated by walking in the heat, getting lost and having various misshapes so I decide to end my suffering and get at the albergue as soon as possible. I ask a taxi driver how much it would cost me to get to Palacio. The driver gets out, talks with other drivers, one comes up with a map and begins to show me what route I should take in order to get there. The ride would cost me 4-5 Euros. The location didn't seem to far away, judging by the map. I walked all day and felt that I could still push myself a little bit more. I ended up taking the map, thanking the taxi drivers for their help and going on my way. I stop at a bench and begin to study the map. I notice that the albergue is actually an albergue juvenil, I came upon one like that in La Isla and I'm definitely not in the age range to classify as a juvenile. On the map at the bus station there is no 'juvenil' mentioned. Damn! What to do now? If I would have taken a taxi I would have wasted five Euros for nothing. And I would also have ended in the opposite direction of the coastline where all the hotels are (and where I would later find accommodation) and would have had to make the road back.

My only option now was to find a hostel. The map has all sorts of things in it but no hostels. Fine, a hotel then. I zero in on two 1 star hotels, looking for the cheapest accommodation. They are close to the El Carmen area which in turn is close to the beach. I begin to walk towards that area. I go through many streets with fancy looking shops and fancy looking people. I felt uneasy and like an alien on the streets. Me, a dirty, limping peregrino with a physical handicap. I finally get to hotel Cape Verde. Price: 31 Euros. It seemed much so I said that I will look around and left. Nearby, I get to hotel Avenida. Price: 28 Euros. I'll take it. It's late, I'm tired, I want to pee, my blisters are getting worse. I resign and I won't be looking no more. I managed to save three Euros anyway. For 28 Euros I get a little room, TV, a bathroom with a shower and a bidet – interesting. The building across has messages referring to the political situation in Venezuela and to the Palestinian cause. I rest a bit. I google and get to the site of the albergue juvenil. The info on the site confirms that I made the right call to abandon the pursuit of it. In need of food, I stroll the streets in search of supermercados. There should be two of them on Portugal street. I find El Arbol with empty counters and not much stuff to chose from. I spend 6 Euros on queso, chorizo, beer, bread and almost 1 kilogram of bananas. Back at the hotel, I have to discard the chorizo, it smelled and tasted like it came through the other end of a person...or animal. I don't want to get food poisoning...again. I take a bath, listen to some music, Pink Floyd – Speak To Me and call it a day!

Day 22, 12 May, Aviles

Started the day being a bit lazy and going out of the hotel room at 8:30 AM. I used yesterdays' map to intersect my steps with the Camino. I got to the beach and from that point I started following the arrows and the shells embedded in the pavement. I must admit, the bronze shells look kinda cool. I keep a fast pace in part due to the fact that my right foot blister healed and in part due to the fact that I wanted to leave the big city as soon as possible. At about 9:30 AM I'm finally out of the city. On my way out I stop at a Discount % supermarket to get some food and a 1.5 liters bottle of water; I hoped to find the sweet Freeway drink again, I've been a fan of it since I had tasted it first time in Potes if I remember correctly, it doesn't contain sugar but it has some artificial sweeteners which give some taste to the water and help with the thirst. Bought 1 queso Gouda, 1 Raviolli, 1 sliced chorizo, almost 1 kilogram of bananas for about 6 Euros in total. I'm glad that I stopped to buy some supplies at that location because there were no other sources of food and water all the way to Aviles. About half of one of the two breads that I strapped to my backpack managed to break off due to the constant movement. Not long after this episode, the arrows point to a dead end somewhere along some train tracks, there was no possible way I could have continued to walk across or to go on train tracks. I take the path up a bridge after a bit of backtracking.

I'm now in the industrial part outside of Gijon. Ocher, xix century looking plants spewing red fumes and steam dot much of the landscape. It's raining but with tiny droplets so I don't bother putting my rain jacket. The hills are foggy, the clouds dark, it looks gloomy and dismal, it reminds me of some scene in Lord of The Rings that happens in Mordor. I decide to have some breakfast at a bus stop near a busy intersection. Roads circulated by trucks, bridges and train tracks all intersect in this point. It's not the best place to eat but at least I have a place to sit down and get out of the rain. I also had to get rid of some weight and the best way to do that is by eating it. While I was eating two German ladies in their red raincoats pass by me. I'm done eating and start getting on the road again. Now starts a steep climb up the hill. I notice that Arcelor Mittal has a presence around these places so I assume that the industry that I'm seeing with all its furnaces and mounds of dirty ore might have something to do with steel. Walking up through a village I pleasantly discover a special place where peregrinos can take water and nourishment in the form of nuts. There is also a sign saying that free lodging is available for tourists at Amada. Nice gesture. There are 16 kilometers more to Aviles. Not far away on the road there are also two chairs posted on each side of a Camino pillar for the weary traveler. The location of the chairs and the sign also marks the end of the steep climb. A horizontal, more or less, pleasant walk starts now. The road is quite good and high hills covered in a thick forest can be observed to the left. At a crossroad the pilgrim has the option to take a detour and go left and visit the San Pablo dolmen or to continue going up the Monte Areo – Aula del Neolitico. I choose not to take the detour given the steep climb that I just did and thinking that I might get another chance to see some neolithic stuff, as advertised on a sign, further down the road – the dolmen is a rock after all and I have no idea how far it is. It didn't happen to be any trace of Neolithic stuff down the road, the path took me down into a valley and into a village. I see in the village an old man wearing wooden shoes in the style of the dutch klompen ones. In the little farming village of Ponte Piedra there is a place where oldtimers would wash their clothes in common. I encounter the two older German ladies again, this time changing places, I am the one who passes by and they are the ones that are eating while sitting on a bench near a nice looking iglesia. The path takes me, again, as what as I perceive as being an u-turn, towards Gijon. I walk across a field. I notice how the freshly cut grass is neatly packed into ballots of hay by a specialized machine.

Close to the highway there is a Hollywood-esque sign of a bull. It's Bullywood, I think. The arrows take me on a highway for the next few kilometers. Another Arcelor Mittal facility, by now AM seems to be like a small kingdom, a country within a country. Kilometer after kilometer, there are never ending industrial facilities, train tracks and trains to feed the hungry plants, numerous big trucks roaming the highway. A sign says Tasona. I check my sheet – there are five kilometers more to Aviles. Maybe an hour more of walking, I think. Beside of the mammoth size industry there is nothing else worth mentioning.

I am trying to keep my spirit up even though my motivation is falling. There are four kilometers more to go. Three kilometers more to go. The buildings are more modest looking than what I'm used to see. It kinda starts reminding me about Eastern Europe and home. The arrows point right towards a bridge. "It might be a detour" I think, but the bridge looks interesting. I go up the bridge and then down. There is a nice promenade along the right side of the river but to the right of the promenade there is industry...spaced only by a fence, a car road and a train track. Heavy industry oozing a heavy smell from time to time is only about 100 meters away. There are ducks in the river. I wonder why the ducks are still staying in this place. I wonder why there are people walking on this promenade given the foul smell. It could have been such a nice place without the industry. The promenade keeps going and going. Through industry now. It gets annoying and I'm starting to lose my temperament. The promenade is called La

Marzaniella I think.

The arrows point up to some stairs and from there towards the center of the city. I'm finally in Aviles. It seems to be a big city and I'm fed up with walking for today and I don't want to repeat the Gijon experience so I'm paying close attention to the signs and hoping that my ordeal will soon end. I walk maybe 500 meters across the city and encounter a sign saying: to the right there is the Camin Del Pelegrin, to the left Agospiu De Pelegrinos. I guess that Agospiu means Albergue. I investigate the left side of my visual field. I'm right in front of the Albergue! Albergue Pedro Solis. Cost: 5 Euros. When the hospitalero guy asked if I'm coming from Xixon (Gijon) I answered Xi instead of Si. Obviously, I was quite distraught by today's experience. There are 48 places here, I see some familiar faces including Godffrey the Australian guy from Villaviciosa. I talked with him about today's experience and some other small talk stuff. He seems to be surviving on fruits and coffee. I rest a bit and then go to hunt for some wine, vino as the Australian guy is saying. I find some Don Luciano red wine at 1.25 Euros. I also buy a small bottle of water – so I can keep the container and use it later, and a Desperados cerveza witch has tequila in it. The name of the supermarket is Alimerka and it's somewhere on the right side of the Camino. It seems to be a bit more expensive than other supermarket chains. A bunch of old French people arrive at the Albergue. They start bringing luggage from outside (the Albergue has an outside court sealed off from the rest of the world by a wall and a door). I can't see it but there might be a support car parked outside. They seem to be the type that send their luggage in front of them at the next stop. There are a lot of them and they are quite loud. It starts raining. Godfrey sees me writing and asks if I'm writing a book.

"Made from the outstanding variety tempranillo, this wine has intense violet and blue notes and combines ripe berry aromas with an elegant touch of young trees. An easy drinking style wine, rich and well-balanced, ideal for the Mediterranean cuisine." It is a nice, smooth and an easy drink indeed. It's my first Desperados beer and I also enjoy it for the smooth taste. Cheers!

There are a lot of people in here and there is a lot of snoring going on, it's like a symphony. Some French guy is moaning in his sleep..."Ay ay ay" with a French accent. He gets up and goes to the bathroom loudly.

Day 23, 13 May, Soto de Liuna

I wake up at 6:30 AM. There are people with headlights on, zipping and unzipping their backpacks and belongings furiously. The guy in the bed next to mine is quite annoying with his headlamp. So inconsiderate. I move my stuff in the kitchen, eat there and leave at 7:00 AM. There are still puddles from the rain last night. I start following the Camino shells through the city, taking pictures of interesting buildings in the process. At one point I lose track of the shells. I thought that they would lead me in a straight direction but they disappeared somewhere to my left most probably. I kept going straight towards the end of the town. Looked attentive after traffic signs; I knew that I can take the N-632 straight to Soto de Luna according to my map of the Asturias. My going in a straight line ends when I encounter the gates of some plant. In some parts of my walk I could still smell the foul odour of industry.

At a bus station I see a lady who is walking her dog and ask her if I'm on a good direction and show her the map. She says yes, says to follow the road which is now turning to the left and to ask people further down the way. Not long after the encounter, I find myself on the road to Salinas; I check my map, the Camino goes through Salinas. I notice that by taking this accidental detour I skipped over the Sabago, San Cristobal, La Sablera "checkpoints" of today's stage. "I might be ahead of schedule", I thought, which is not bad considering the fact that Aviles – Soto de Luna is one of the longest stages of the Camino totaling about 42 kilometers. All the map checking and the constant looking for a trace of the Camino was quite an ongoing mental undertaking. It's much easier to follow some arrows like a sheep than to worry at every step if you are on the right track.

Today's road would be a long one, there is no time for wrong turns, constant map checks and guesswork. Checking my sheet again I realize that I've seen a traffic sign saying San Cristobal about 50 meters back. I decide to turn back, see the sign again, head to San Cristobal and try to find the Camino there. I go uphill, see two unofficial looking arrows; there are now three possible routes, all leading uphill, which one should I take? There are no other arrows besides the ones on the wall. I decide to go with the path that is advertised by a sign as Cristobal (entrevista). I walk on the street dotted with houses in each side and...nothing. No other signs at all. I'm beginning to think that going on this route is a bad idea, maybe I should just go back towards the road to Salinas and follow the N-632 from there. I notice another settlement, not far away, on the left side of the hill; I decide to go there and to ask and find out where I am. However, on the road towards it, I encounter the Camino arrows and the official pillar. The 'A pie' (on foot) route goes through the forest, the 'Bicl' (on bike) route goes through the way that I just came from. Those arrows on the wall make sense now, they were for the people that are doing the Camino on bike. Thus, I start following the Camino again and let my mind off the constant guesswork.

I soon find myself walking through urban areas with nice houses and clean streets. There are some names, I check them against my map and the sheet but I find no matches. I encounter my first peregrinos and pass them somewhere on a hill. A limping man and a chubby lady. Somewhere near Piedra – on the map it's Piedrablancas (it's not the first time when I find such differences), the path starts to get less urban and more rural with green pastures and forests dotting the landscape. There are plenty of airplanes landing and taking off, I must be close to the airport that is marked on the map. A quite long walk through the forest puts me in a good mood. The road goes now towards the valley bellow and through a village. I make a short stop at a water source and fill my only 0.5 liters bottle. The path makes an u-turn up the hill and then down again through a forest. The road is muddy and full of stones that I have to avoid. While walking slowly downhill I get passed by the two Spanish guys, the umbrella guy and the bald with glasses guy, they seem to walk nonchalantly in their sport shoes, floating across the rocks. I'm starting to think that I don't have enough padding because I'm feeling every rock. Maybe I should have come with my running shoes instead of my trekking shoes. I pass by a limping Spanish guy, I ask him if he is OK, he says no and shows his foot...he didn't knew the right word for his condition, I say shin and show at my leg, he says "no...water", "Ah, blisters?" "Yes! Four of them!".

The road goes now through a grassy track, it's not properly marked and the two Spanish who are now ahead of me have to come back after a third Spanish guy shouts and tells them that they took a wrong turn. The shell is on an electrical pillar, the path is towards the highway and the hill, not to the left. Making my way up the hill I find myself on Calle Del Peregrino in El Castillo. I guess it's named this way after the fortress with the big walls which can be seen from the top of the hill. Nice view of the big river, there are some boats in it. The ocean is not far.

The road goes through an urban area. I notice a nice open garden with beautiful flowers on the right side of the street, on the left side there is a dump and garbage. I guess that each balances the other out. The road makes a new u-turn and I'm heading now back to the fortress and El Castillo. I get to a bridge crossing and notice the limping Spanish guy going slowly across the bridge. He must have taken a shortcut by following the N-632. Somewhere near Muros I also decide to follow the N-632, otherwise, the Camino would have taken me up a steep hill and down intersecting again with the N-632 highway. Soon after, the Camino goes to the right, up a village this time. I chose to ignore the Camino again and to continue on the main highway. I get to a El Arbol supermarket. For 3.56 Euros I buy: 0.64 kilograms of bananas, 1.5 liters of Gaseosa Dia water 0.28 Euros, queso Gouda 1.19 Euros, chorizo Lonch-Dia 1.29 Euros. I stop in the parking lot for a lunch. I notice two peregrinos coming on the N highway and continuing until they disappear somewhere to the right. I finish my lunch and follow them. Apparently, I can't escape the arrows, wherever I go I keep on seeing them...and following them.

I cross the little city of Muros. There are plenty of peregrinos and tourists staying at the bars. There is a caravan with a NL number on it, it seems that there are Dutch tourists everywhere I go. Casa Consistorial built in 1876 looks interesting. I like these kind of old buildings. I see some walls, maybe there is another castle? At the exit out of Muros I encounter the other Australian guy from yesterday's albergue, sitting and drying his socks. "Good idea", I think, "I should do the same thing, change or dry my socks during the day". This should prevent blisters or at least make their presence less likely.

A new walk across yet another eucalyptus forest. Mud and rocks. The Australian passes by me saying "A good day for a walk". He seems to walk effortless across the rocks. He also has running shoes. I can now see the ocean through the canopy. I'm thinking that I'm still close to the beach, according to the map Soto de Liuna is more inland and this means one thing: I still have more to go. I try to keep up with the Australian but to no avail. I enter an urbanized area again. There are fancy buildings. I'm in Cudillero now. I take a pic of a Guardia Civil headquarter. I think that I see at a terrace cafe a guy from the albergue sitting and relaxing (the guy would get ahead of me to Soto, by taking the N-632 shortcut I guess). I walk and then walk some more. Somewhere near a tall and long bridge I have to walk downhill in serpentines towards the beach. I pass hotel Marina, think that at this point many peregrinos might just give up and check in, and then go up yet another hill.

After reaching the bridge level, on the other side this time, I am faced with a masochistic portion of the road full of gravel, small rocks...I can't avoid anything and have to go through the mine field. I curse the Camino and slowly limp my way through it. I've already walked so much today...and now this. But now I've crossed the main A-8 highway, the bridge and finally started going inland. Soto de Liuna shouldn't be far away according to my map. I'm starting to think that today was the toughest day of the Camino so far, a lot of kilometers, u-turns and plenty of hills to climb. And lets not forget the quality of the roads. I was starting to get frustrated.

I'm going through the forest again, and again, it seems like I'm going backwards because the road is doing an u-turn. While crossing a sparse village a small dog comes after me and tries to bite the sole of my shoe, I curse him and try to kick him but he is more agile than me and runs away. Fifty meters down the road another dog, a big one this time, barks at me. Luckily he is chained. I get an adrenaline rush from these man versus wild encounters and the adrenaline pump keeps me going. I have the impression that this village is Soto de Liuna and I'm looking for the albergue. It turns out that it's not it. Another walk through the forest, this time downhill, through mud...again. I can see through the canopy a cluster of houses at the foothill and the highway. I'm thinking that this should be it. Soto de Liuna is on N-632. This should be it! I descend from the forest and onto the highway. In distance, a sign is saying: Soto de Liuna. I can't believe it, I've made it. It's 17:11PM and I've been walking for ten long hours taking only a few very short breaks, totaling to less than thirty minutes, maybe twenty, in total. I go to another El Arbol shop, buy another 1.5 liter bottle of Gaseosa water and ask where is the albergue, "At the end of the road, first to the right, amarillo building". I get there at 17:30. The hospitalero is not there but he will come at 19:30 the people tell me. With or without hospitalero I proceed to do like everybody else and find myself a bed.

There are unfamiliar faces at the albergue, a girl asks me from where I've came, "Aviles, and you?" "Muros de...N...", I check my sheet "Muros de Nalon?"

"Yes". The headlamp bastard seems to be here. A guy from Germany with dreadlocks sits at a table and moving around him is his dog Pumba. It seems that he adopted the dog on the Camino. He talks with another German guy and from their conversation I learn that he plans to return back on foot to Germany from Finisterre. Apparently, he hid 6000 kilometers of the Camino in five years with no money. The hospitalero arrives, tells me to go and pay 5 Euros and get a stamp at the Ecu bar near the iglesia. It's heavily raining now with small droplets. I get to the bar, pay, and stamp my passport. On the way back I stop at the El Arbol to get a San Miguel beer and a bread. I show the ticket to the hospitalero and he is happy now. There were lots of peregrinos at the bar.

The hospitalero said that the albergue in Pinera is closed...so the plan would be to reach Villar, which is about 36 kilometers from here. It's pouring rain now with small drops, the hills are covered in a white mist. Tomorrow will be mud!

Day 24, 14 May, Villar (Almuna)

There is snoring and farting going on all night long at the albergue. The headlamp bastard is up early again and he is next to me, so it's a 6:30 AM wake again. I do some eating and a few minutes past 7 AM I'm out. I turn back about 100 meters down the road where I've seen some arrows yesterday. I follow them and end up at the albergue. Damn, I walked in a circle. Then I see another, new set of arrows that I start to not follow. I get on the highway instead. My today's plan would be to just follow the highway. After a few minutes on the highway, the drizzle of rain turns into a dense shower with small droplets. The Camino road through the hills and the forests must be exceptionally muddy with all the rain that poured last night and that is continuing to pour even now. It's time to change my clothes for some waterproof ones like my light running hoodie and to cover my backpack with a green, waterproof membrane. Not long after, I see two peregrinos coming out of the forest canopy via the Camino route and hoping onto the highway. I keep following them until the yellow arrows split the path in two, one of them being the Costa route. I remember the hospitalero saying that I should take the Costa route. We all did that.

In the next village the arrows started on a new path away from the highway; I wanted to stay on the highway but I noticed that the highway seemed to go in a curve and the Camino to just cut straight through the valley. The decision was between walking more on an even terrain or to walk less down and up a hill. I'm now in a forest following the two guys and the official Camino. Rocks, mud, a river of mud in fact...I pass a peregrino that seems to be the headlamp bastard. The path is narrow and not a lot of room to maneuver so it's hard to avoid stepping into puddles of water and mud. The course of a little stream coming down the road and the hill seemed to be the most walkable because the water cleared everything in its path leaving only firm ground and rocks. Yes, I'm glad that I'm walking on rocks now.

I'm out of the forest now and back into a new village, Novellana. The story repeats itself, I follow the arrows through the village again, they take me downhill through a lush, green coastal rainforest. The sight is mesmerizing and I enjoy the forest walk immensely. I shot a video. A steep climb to the highway again and to a new village Castaneras. In Castaneras I follow the arrows leading to the playa. I see one of the morning's peregrinos turning back. I ask him why and he says that it looks too steep. He shows me his guidebook in German, I say that I will check and see where the road leads. Twenty meters farther on the road, I have a good view of what is in store for me. It looked steep indeed. I think that the German is right so it's better to go this time on the highway even though it would mean a doing few kilometers more of walking. It's not a good time to go to the beach anyway. It's heavily pouring rain. I guess that my two walks through the rainforest, which was a pleasurable experience, should suffice for today. I keep following the highway. There is mist and the dense rain makes it hard to see what's after a couple of hundreds of meters.

Somewhere after Santa Marina, one can see two huge, long bridges. The highway curves and at the curve I begin to find my first raspberries of the day. They are quite tasty and they are already washed by the rain, the moisture on them also helps to quench my thirst. I'm in good spirits. I now see this pouring rain as an interesting change to my daily routine since I haven't experienced so much rain on the Camino yet. I'm thinking at various things. Thinking that my companeros from the first days of walking have already passed through these places. I'm walking on their footsteps. An interesting thought...to walk on the footsteps of someone else. What were they thinking, what were they doing? Nowadays, my thoughts are centered on the Camino: past experiences, interesting people and conversations that I had with them, present experiences. The Camino is my new reality in which I live the moment, day by day. I'm thinking at funny stuff. Asturias – paraiso natural. It's just another day in Paradise for me! Even though it's pouring rain and I'm starting to get cold. I'm thinking of Russell Hantz, one of the best contestans on the Reality-TV show Survivor, and his words "it's only water", "this is the man test", "if it rains for seven days and for seven nights...I will take it".

At some point, in some village (thankfully I know at least where I am due to the fact the name of the location is written somewhere, there were times when I had no idea through what place I was going) I see the dreadlocked German guy reading a book peacefully and sitting on a bench at a bus station, next to him is Pumba sitting quietly and not moving a muscle, a veritable stone Sphynx. Ballota, Tablizio, Ribon. I get to Cadavedo at about 12:30 PM. I was hungry, a bit cold, the water got into my shoes, onto my map. Think it's about time to find an albergue, I can get to Villar tomorrow after all. While searching for the arrows and the albergue I see the German guy carrying a bolsa full of goodies. Says he went to a supermarket, there is one about 100 meters to the left from where he came. I ask him about the albergue, he pulls his guidebook, takes a look and says that it's somewhere out of Cadavedo, a few hundred meters to the right. Says that he will continue the road to Luarca. I say that there is an albergue in Villar which is about one kilometer before Luarca. He shows me his guidebook and a map that reveals that is not much more distance left to Luarca, "Maybe 12 kilometers". Says it's not even 13:00 PM yet, it's about 12:30 in fact and there is plenty of time left in the day. Made me change my mind so I decide to push myself a bit to get to Villar. "See you later!" When I read and said Jacobsweg in German he asked me where I'm from. "Romania", "Cool! I'm half German and half French".

I get to a supermarket called Unpar or something like that. There I spend 3.75 Euros in heavy coins on : Crik Crok chips – 1 Euro, a 200 gr. Little box of jellies – 1 Euro, Asturias milk – 0.75 Euros, 4 chocolate doughnuts – 1 Euro. I asked myself why I haven't integrated milk in my morning breakfast, it's cheap, it's a source of hydration, it has calories and proteins. It's an easy meal basically. I drink the milk and gobble up the doughnuts on my way out of Cadavedo. A few more hours and I'm done for today. I pass by a bar where a group of "cowboys" vacheros arrived on their horses. They parked their horses on a pasture nearby. They seem to be some kind of tourists, horseback tourists. There are 12 kilometers more to Luarca. Not bad, maybe two hours more of walking. I suddenly get an urgent need to go to the bathroom. I think that there is always something that comes in order to make my day more challenging. I was doing pretty well for today so far in spite of the rain. I try to hold it in and to accelerate my pace. Not far from Canero, I find a good spot and decide to take care of my urgent business. I pass a bridge, to my right, another big bridge for the A-8 highway…"I've seen a lot of those bridges". An abandoned house.

  Ten kilometers more to Luarca. I start digging in my jellies. On my way up the highway serpentine – the highway is called now E-7/N-634 I think – I see a peregrino covered in a red raincoat slowly crossing the road like a Sasquatch and coming from a hike through the forest and disappearing into the canopy again. The Camino route seemed to cut a path right through the hill, the highway seemed to go in circles up the hill. I made the right choice by taking the Camino because the taken path it would prove to be shorter indeed even though steeper. I'm now on a road which is delimited by the big E-7/A-8 highway with a fence. I might have ended on the big highway if I would have kept my course and that would have been a problem because these kind of highways are usually restricted for walkers like me. I would have to backtrack just like I did on day 20 on the way to Villaviciosa. I follow the red Sasquatch on the Camino path which cuts through fields and forests and it's much shorter than the route on the highway.

  Sasquatch disappears somewhere to the right. The Camino is also going to the right, however, there are some arrows and an A symbol suggesting that an albergue is straight ahead (by following the highway in a long straight ling for a few kilometers). I follow this alternative route and get to an intersection...I haven't seen any new arrows so far...hmm...so I decide to keep going even though the traffic signs show that I'm heading towards the center of Luarca. I don't think that is what I want. According to my sheet Villar is 1 kilometer before Luarca. I do a stop, check my sheet...Barcia, Villar. The road to Barcia was a few hundred meters back and going to the right. I check my watch and it's around 16:00 PM. I still have time. I wonder how many places and how many peregrinos there are at the albergue.

On my way back this young guy starts speaking to me. "Albergue?" "Si" I reply. Says that he knows where it is, says that he is a relative of the hospitalero. I believe him even though his appearance seemed to indicate the fact that he is a punk...earrings, face scars, he looked like a South American, maybe Mexican, thug. I think that he might lure me to a back alley and pull a knife on me. I was ready for anything to happen. I follow him for a while on the highway from behind. A lot of cars, including a Guardia Civil one, pass us from the opposite direction. We don't do much talking, he doesn't know English and I'm not that great in Spanish. I'm thinking now that he might not pull a knife on me, maybe just lure me to a more expensive accommodation place like a Casa Rural or something like that. I guess that this is his job...to stroll the highway looking for lost peregrinos like me. I see the Franco-German guy coming in my direction from some street to the right. Says the Albergue is somewhere to the right than to the left a few hundreds meters, I don't get his directions too well. He was heading to the Alimerka supermarket nearby. I want to go on the street that he came from, explain it to the Spanish guy. We keep talking, I insisting to go to the right, he insisting to go to the left, when I get the impression that I see some yellow stuff on the street (highway) some twenty meters ahead. Turns out that the yellow stuff are yellow arrows. There is an Albergue to the left 400 meters away. I begin to trust the guy. He says that there are two albergues, a private one which costs 5 Euros and the Municipal one which costs 10 Euros.

I finally get there. Turns out that the hospitalero is his dad. I'm the only one staying at the albergue. I fill out the accommodation forms while the hospitalero dries my peregrino passport in the microwave oven. "La lluvia" I explained about the wetness of my passport. He doesn't have change for 50 Euros. He tells me that I can change at the Alimerka and that he will take me there with his car. I go to my room, get my valuables so that I don't leave them behind – I still couldn't fully trust his son. I hop in the car and we get to the supermarket. The dreadlocks guy is nonchalantly sitting with a beer in his hand, rested against the outside wall of the building. I don't see Pumba. I have no idea how he got ahead of me...again, I never saw him pass me. He is staying like he is waiting for something to happen. I have the impression somehow that he is begging...or was begging (it would later prove that he is indeed a beggar, after all, he travels without money). He seems to act as he doesn't sees me, even though he definitely saw me get out of the car, like he is ashamed that he is staying there or something like that...I never had spoken to the guy, only saw him at the albergue and overheard his conversation so I decided to ignore him as well. At Alimerka I spend 5.90 Euros on: Bread, 340 gr. - 0.60 Euros, 1 liter of El Aguila Negra cerveza – 1 Euro, 1.5 liters of Gaseosa water – 0.26 Euro, Leche Alimerka milk – 0.59 Euros, sliced Gouda cheese – 1.45 Euros, sliced Salchichon – 1 Euro, sliced Pamplona chorizo – 1 Euro. Again, Alimerka seems to be more expensive than the alternatives. The hospitalero salutes the people around, is recognized by various people, helps me around with the shopping, offers to carry my bag. We get back into the car and we start searching for the Franco-German guy. His son noticed our conversations and told the father about my amigo so the father is now determined to reunite the 'friends' and to gain another customer as well. The Franco-German is nowhere to be seen, not at Alimerka, not on the way to the albergue, nowhere. I'm not that determined to find him but the hospitalero is, he works hard for another five potential Euros and is even risking some fuel. We get all the way to Luarca, roam the streets of the nearby Barcia (I think) and return back empty handed from the manhunt. I get a glimpse of Luarca and it looks like a very nice little fishing town.

When we arrive at the albergue, the Franco-German is already there. Since there is nobody else there I get to talk with him and get to know him better. He says that he is doing the Camino in stages and this is his forth time (stage) on the Camino. He likes to walk alone, walks a few days and then he goes back. These are the days when he gets tranquility and solitude. I tell him about some of my experiences so far, about the Camino Lebaniego. He laughs maniacally at jokes or at things that are not actually funny. I'm trying to be extra funny today just to see his maniac laugh. We talk about today's experience about the guy with the dreadlocks – he also noticed him today and yesterday. The dreadlocked hippie tries to get in the albergue but is not permitted because of his dog. While getting my shoes off I notice that my feet look like they've been sitting in a bathtub for two hours. The albergue costs five Euros and it's not much of an albergue but the hospitalero is quite helpful. Two other Spanish chicas come and check in, I have seen them yesterday at the albergue.

My feet throbbed with pain all night long, I couldn't go to sleep but the exhaustion finally beats the pain. In the morning my feet still looked like they stayed in a bathtub for hours, still shriveled and still hurting. It wasn't a good idea to push myself and to beat my wet feet. Turns out that there is no actual Villar around here, I'm actually in the small settlement of Almuna. My sheet seems to indicate the presence of the ghost location of Villar.

Day 25, 15 May, La Caridad

Woke up at past 7:30 AM. The German left after about 20 minutes, I went out of the albergue at 8:47 AM. The Spanish chicas seem to have "borrowed" all the toilet paper. I follow the the arrows until I have a great view of the city of Luarca from a high vantage point. I slowly walk across Luarca, admiring the buildings and the narrows streets. Following the Camino out of Luarca I get lost at some point in an area close to San Martin because of a badly placed shell sign which is invisible for the walker going on the inside part of the road curvature. I have seen the yellow, red and blue colors on a post but thought that they are irrelevant to the Camino. A sign with "Museo Rural" in yellow seemed to indicate the right way. I see a sign advertising a camping place; I am inclined to follow it and to take a rest for the day and to rest my aching feet. At this point I'm thinking more at sparing myself the effort than pushing myself again. It's not worth spending a night in agony and having trench foot in the morning just to do another 10-15 kilometers for the day.

I see two pilgrim-looking silhouettes walking on a road which is across the field. I didn't wanted to go across the field so I went ahead with the intent of taking side roads to the right leading to villas but decide to track back after noticing that San Martin seemed to be off-course according to my map. Of course that I'm frustrated at this point, getting lost and limping are no ingredients for happiness. On my way back I notice two elderly gentlemen coming from the opposite way. I see their backpacks and I think that they are heading to the camping site. I don't warn them about the lure of the Museo Rural which was, by the way, closed and didn't seemed to be worth visiting.

The Camino leads me to an old and derelict church site that it seems to have served as a hospital during the

Spanish flu. I wander cautiously around the site a bit with the hope that I won't catch the flu. I get back to walking and after a short while I make a stop at a bench situated on a lonely rural road. The two elderly gentlemen pass by me while I am sitting. They are casually dressed with shirts, dock pants but with hiking boots and backpacks. They look like two old hipsters. One of them is sporting an epic Hemingway-esque beard.

While going across a small village I suddenly hear a loud detonation coming from somewhere nearby to the left. Sounded like a cannon that fired a blank projectile. The sound goes cracking into distance. Two more detonations. I'm under bombardment now. On my left there is a live, green wall so I can't see what is going on and to the right there is a vast empty field. I continue walking while looking for the source of the thunderous sounds. At the next house I see a guy in blue overalls slowly closing a metal sliding door in front of him. He waves his hand in the form of a salute. I wave back. Almost one hour later I would hear the thunderous sound two more times. My guess would be that it's an anti-crow sort of wonder weapon.

In the small village of Carral I see an interesting garden with flowers and pottery in the shape of various cartoon characters. In El Rellon I see a vase with a crusade theme on it. While walking on a road adjacent to a field I observe how a specialized machine on wheels cuts the grass. I slowly climb up the hill. On the rocky, quarry-looking top of the hill I see the Australian guy waving his socks in the air and blowing air on them. I stop in order to have a chat with him. I say that it's a good idea, in regard to what he is doing, he replies saying that he repeats the process once every three hours. I tell him about my experience on the Camino Lebaniego. On the way down the rocky hill a dog suddenly comes next and close to me right under my hand, freaking me out. "What the f...'. Coming after the dog, the owner says "I'm sorry'. I haven't heard them coming.

From the hill top I could see a cluster of houses on the next hill which seemed to be Navia, the final point of today's journey. I have a chat with Peter the Australian plumber all the way to the entry of the village of Navia (presumably). I tell him about Romania, about the Carpathian mountains, about prices, I ask him if he feels like home given all the eucalyptus trees that we see around and he says that yes, the eucalyptus trees grow here faster than in Australia because they have better conditions, said that he saw some pretty thick ones too. I jokingly said that only koalas are missing from the landscape. Said about the many bridges dotting the landscape that they are quite a feat of engineering. Said that this Camino is his first and last one, that he will go to England afterwards and walk it coast to coast. While on the highway, he kept walking backwards and facing me, exposing himself to the risk of getting hit by a car. He is a plumber, doing a job that takes him many times outdoors. "Not bad" I think about the outdoors activity, I am tempted to do a more outdoorsy kind of work instead of having to sit in front of a computer a large part of the day. I stop to take some pics of an interesting house with all sorts of statues and toys put on a display in a small yard. Peter is a fast walker so he gains distance. Getting into this new location which I thought to be Navia, I wanted to ask someone what is the name of this settlement. I find my answer sooner than expected, Villapedre. Damn.

There is still a lot more to go until Navia, seven kilometers. The pensions and the accommodations that I see around Villapedre look expensive so I keep pushing on. No trace of an albergue. Getting out of Villapedre I notice a graffiti with a Revolucion and Save Donbass theme. Peter is coming from the opposite side of the highway. He is followed by a man. It seems that he took a wrong turn. The arrows are pointing to the right and out of the highway, he continued walking straight ahead on the highway. "I know people that have guidebooks and they are getting lost more frequent than me" he joked around. In Pinera the albergue was indeed closed just like the hospitalero from Soto de Luna said it would be. It's in renovation until November 2016. It's an albergue that in a former life was a school just like the one in La Fuente or the one in Islares which was a kindergarten. The small villages are getting depopulated with the elderly being the ones who remained behind. I noticed this phenomena while walking on the Camino Lebaniego with its small sparse villages. Who knows how many people will be left in these villages in the next 10, 20, 30 years? What kind of experience will the peregrino have while going through empty settlements? A lonely one for sure.

The Camino takes me through a bit of welcomed

shade in the form of a small wooded area. The little forest has a spring that goes through it and the spring has a marshy area along it. It's not easy to avoid the mud or the water but I finally do it and I'm now crossing straight through fields and villages while being followed by the two elderly Frenchmen. In La Colorada I notice a Roca factory. "Wait, where have I seen this name before? Hmm...I know! It's on every toilet that I've seen so far in Spain. Roca is a maker of toilets." I'm exited about this discovery for some reason, it's the feeling that you get when you see a celebrity.

At the entry point of Navia the Camino literally takes you to the cemetery. Camino, are you hinting towards something? Coming down from the cemetery I get a good view of the city of Navia. Not bad looking! My hopes are up. I navigate through the seemingly depopulated city and because today is Sunday most of the places are closed and there are no cheap looking hotels. And no supermercados. I leave Navia. The two old Frenchmen were scrambling across the city looking for something, accommodation I guess. I thought that maybe I can find some open shops in the urban area that continues out of Navia and after a bridge. I was right and did find something but the problem was that the owner won't let you navigate the isles. Seriously. "No, no...say and I will go and bring it" you can look but you can't touch. I can't even see the products if I have to stay at the counter. I don't have time for stupid things like these, this is a deal breaker for me so I leave the shop. On my way up the Barqueiros hill I feel that I am too hungry to continue so I stop and devour some of the bread that I was carrying and gobbled it down with aqua gaseosa. In Jarrio I stop in order to do a sock and shoe drying session. The promenade on the hilltop overlooking Jarrio was quite pleasant. On a field nearby I notice something that looked like a bird of prey circling over.

I trek towards the coast when I suddenly see a sign saying Cartavio. Nice! A little bit more to go and I'm done. About four kilometers more or less to go (to Arboces). I follow the arrows that deceptively take me through detours off the main highway into small settlements around it. I am starting to get really frustrated by all of it: the hunger, the blisters, the limping, the gravel roads, the "Spanish kilometers", the little but many other things like getting lost, being bombarded, depopulated settlements and closed shops, inaccurate information, silly shop policies and ninja dogs.

In Arboces it didn't turn out to be any albergue, only a camping site, some 300 meters right from the highway. The hospitalero in Almuna must have been wrong when he told us about an albergue in Arboces. I get to a sign saying Albergue – 2 kilometers, think that is maybe a 20 minutes walk and finally get there.

There, at the albergue in La Caridad, I find the Franco-German and some other people. I was last to arrive there, at about 19:00 PM. All the lower places in the bunk beds are occupied and even some of the upper beds. I haven't eaten in a long time. Staying at the albergue costs 5 Euros. The hospitalero is Jose Antonio Garcia, a guy who is the only survivor of a shipwreck and who did over 100000 kilometers around the world on foot. I shake his hands and give him a hug and tell him that I have seen a news print with him back in La Isla. I went straight to the Porchias restaurant bar along with most of the other people from the albergue. I have two beers and a "pilgrim's menu" for 9 Euros: spaghetti with sauce, fries, 4-5 big pieces of chicken meat. I take a photo with Jose. While staying at the bar and enjoying my meal I listened to his conversation with other Spanish guys. From what I understood, he was laughing about some of the peregrinos, about some German woman, trying to impress the little crowd of young guys around him. He was showing them news about him on his phone. He was saying about a Rumeno, who came in last and who is educated, unlike other disrespectful, uneducated peregrinos. He was obviously talking about me but didn't knew that I'm sitting beside him – he was staying with his back facing toward me. Jose is broke, he sleeps in a tent nearby the albergue (I initially thought that it is the tent of a peregrino), has various newspaper clippings about his adventures written in various languages. He might be broke but I guess that in his ten years of constant adventure he lived as for several lives...maybe the satisfaction is greater for him rather than having a career and a dull life.

I go straight to bed after dinner. I can't sleep too well with all the snoring and movements around me.

I tried finding more informations on the Internet about Jose Antonio Garcia. He has a common Spanish name and is mostly known in his country so it's hard to come up with articles in English about him. I quote from http://www.odditycentral.com/news/the-pilgrim-man-spends-eleven-years-walking-107000-kilometers-in-the-name-of-faith.html

"Born in Puerto de Santa María, in the Spanish province of Cadiz, Jose Antonio Garcia spent most of his life on water, working as a sailor. He wasn't the most religious person, but after going through a near-death experience, he decided to dedicate his life to an epic pilgrimage to as many holy sites as he could walk to. In 1999, the fishing boat Jose was working on capsized off the coast of Norway, and he was the only survivor out of a crew of 17. He spent hours in the freezing water clinging to the bodies of two fellow sailors, and it was then that he turned to religion, vowing to the Virgen del Carmel, the patron of sailors, that he would walk to all of the world's holy shrines, if she saved his life.

Miraculously, Jose was found by a rescue team, but had to spend the next eight months in a hyperbaric chamber to recover from his injuries. But even after that long period of time, he was still unable to walk, and doctors were unsure that he would ever be able to use his legs again. Garcia spent the next two years in a wheelchair, and two more after that walking with crutches, but in the end, he was able to walk like a normal person again. And he never forgot the promise he made to the Virgen del Carmen when he was so close to death. As soon as he was back on his feet, he took out his life savings (around 36,000 euros), filled up a backpack with basic travel items, and left his home town to visit as many

holy sites as he could."
Very impressive story!

Day 26, 16 May, Ribadeo

Woke up early, largely because of the early and loud headlamp wearing kind of guys. Not having much to pack and nothing to eat I was out of the albergue's door by 6:40 AM. Today's journey was relatively easy, there are about 20 kilometers in this stage, not much hill climbing, most of the road consisted of straight lines and the Camino didn't detoured from the highway...that much. Around 8:40 AM I was at the outskirts of Tapia De Casariego, I tried shopping at an Alimerka supermarket but it was not opened yet, of course, it's too early for them. In Romania, and in most of the other countries in this world I guess, it would have already been open for more than an hour. I follow most of the Camino trails. Walked on the highway at a fast pace. In Porcia I notice two little goats eating grass and other vegetation. They leaped on a rock wall when I passed by. Apparently, I've been walking on the Ruta Del Ferro y Del Oro. I have no idea why it's called that way, I've seen iron but no gold. The Camino takes you through rural villages and through cultivated fields. From time to time a lonely passing tractor can be seen on the road; or a car; or elderly people walking at a fast pace in the morning. Sometimes you can estimate the size of the next city by the number of people that you see walking, running or cycling on promenades outside of it (at any hour).

A lonely iglesia staying in the middle of the green field. The dark clouds in the sky have an ominous presence. The darkness creates an interesting, contrasting image. The church turns out to be a cemetery. In Tapia De Casariego I realized that I'm about halfway the distance to Ribadeo. I asked myself why the Camino is taking us on what seemed to be like a loop around the highway. I found a clue in the neatly designed sign that lets the traveler know that Tapia is only 1000 meters away: a beach. Coming from the walking promenade the peregrino is suddenly hit with an amazing view of the playa. Coastal rocks, the green of the moss and the algae, a cave which almost made me visit it if it wasn't so hard to cross plenty of sharp and slippery rocks down a cliff in order to get to it. Ribeiro de Represas.

The albergue is right next to the playa, it has an excellent view and benches. If it would have been yesterday's situation (thinking about sparring my aching feet) I would have lodged in right away. I pass by a house with two cats on its roof. I try to take a pic but the cats that were standing still like veritable statues suddenly decide to disappear. I pass by a market. At a stand there were scythes and other pointy and cutting tools like, for example, an Arabic looking dagger. At a fruit stand I ask for the price of the platanos and it's 1.77 Euros. A bit pricey. I notice huge, red, delicious looking cherries, would have liked to buy but I didn't wanted to load myself again like I've done in the past. Now, writing these lines while sitting comfortable on a chair back home it doesn't seem to be a good argument in favor of ditching those tasty looking cherries. I can assure the reader that at some point, on the Camino, one can even negatively feel the impact of the weight of some heavy coins in the pocket. Of course, how much you are already carrying also counts. I was carrying more than ten percent than my body weight. Where did I got this figure from? The people on the Camino were saying that is not recommended to carry more than ten percent of your body weight.

After about 20 meters from the market there is a small Carniceria type of shop where I buy four chocolate cupcakes for 1 Euro, Asturias milk and chorizo for 1.75 Euros, in total 2.75 Euros. I start eating the cakes and drinking the milk when I notice Peter the Australian coming on the road with a little bag of fruits (from the nearby market I presume). We talk about various stuff like: he googled about Romania the day before after saying in our previous conversation that he will do so, about running, it seems that he is also a runner, he did the New York marathon (50000 participants, many tourists who walk in the middle of the running crowd, four hours spent in the cold while going through security checks), and the Canberra and Vancouver ones, about food, said that people in Australia are obese, I told him that the Romanians are also getting fatter since the fall of Communism. He asked me if we have a national military service in Romania, said that I speak a good English, I replied that unfortunately we are mostly taught French in schools. He has a quick pace so I fasten mine up in order to keep up with him; it wasn't easy and I started to break a sweat. Peter is wearing a large white hat (and told him about the Austrian guy's hat which was similar), a T-shirt and short pants. His backpack doesn't seem to be heavy, he is carrying running shoes and hiking boots. I tell him that I bought my trekking shoes for about $20, he replied that his cost $250 but at least they don't let the water in. We talk about Romanian stray dogs and the fact that many of them are adopted by Europeans. This led to an interesting topic. It seemed that while staying in the Philippines he was faced with the situation of eating a dog, it's a place where they eat only dogs he says. Also in the Philippines, he asked for an egg and got a balut instead which is an egg that contains the developing embryo of a bird.

We talk about the life on the Camino and how other pilgrims take the train or other shortcuts. At an intersection, two Germans were sitting, studying their guidebooks and maps and trying to figure out something. The Camino markings are obvious, anyone can easily see them...and it's also obvious that the Germans were looking for some shortcut. Peter also remarked the Camino detours that take you through various little villages. I say "that's because it's an itinerario cultural", he replies saying that "after a while they all begin to seem the same, it's like Groundhog day, did you see the movie?" "The one with Bill Murray? Yeah!". It's true, after a while it does seem like Groundhog Day.

With a pacemaker and an interesting and funny conversation going on I seem to just fly through places, places that seem to get redundant after a while. We get to the Pinaronda beach which is absolutely beautiful.

There is an arrow pointing a way through a marshy, high-grass type of landscape, a few meters ahead, there is a another sign, a bit less visible, pointing to a wooden platform above the marsh and an easy, walkable path. "The dumb way and the smart way" says Peter. We take the path on the wooden platform. Close by and behind us, the two Germans take the marsh path. "The Germans took the dumb path! No wonder why they don't win many wars!"

We stop at a nearby bus station which is actually a little covered bench and some flimsy walls on three sides. A few meters across, a sign tells us that we are in Figueras. Not bad, there are about two kilometers more to go! We pull off our shoes and socks for a drying session. I ask him where did he learned this method. "I made blisters while walking the first stage from Irun to San Sebastian, I never had blisters wearing my running shoes. This Dutch lady punctured my blisters and left a bit of cotton inside the blisters so it can keep sucking up the fluid." I finish eating my chocolate cakes and drink all the milk, he eats his fruits and peanuts. The Germans pass us one by one, smiling in the process. We get ready to go. "We've got some Germans to catch!" says Peter. Somewhere out of Figueras I find some bins in which I throw my garbage. While the garbage bag was going into the darkness of the bin I see the package of the sliced chorizo caserole through the bag. Damn, I forgot that there was still some chorizo left in it. The bin is too deep to start dumpster diving. I must carry on. Not far away, we get to a sign that tells us that Puente de Los Santos comes next. It's a 600 meters long bridge. The view of Ribadeo, the huge bridge, the ocean, the little town of Castropol on one side of the river, green waters, the breeze, the height. I take some pics and a do a short video.

The arrows take us under the bridge and they disappear at some point. We get to the center of Ribadeo. The impressive, big church-looking building that I saw from the other side of the river, turns out not to be a church. The town looks deserted at its periphery with empty streets and closed shops. It's not even 13:00 PM yet. Peter wants to go farther than Ribadeo. The information center is closed. He writes down his email address, says that we might see each other in Australia – or in New Zealand – or on the tracks of the Camino. I notice a map posted on a board outside of the info center and I locate the albergue which is situated somewhere around the bridge. I part ways with Peter. On my way back to the bridge I notice a little sign saying Fruteria. The little shop is across a park where little kids are playing ball and old people are sitting on benches. I go inside and end up spending 14 Euros on: 3 Desperados beers – 3.60 Euros, milk – 0.79 Euros, Oreos – 1.49 Euros, queso Semi Graso – 4.21 Euro, Mortadella Siciliana – 2 x 1.5 Euros each, and a bread.

I finally manage to find the albergue. It opens at 14:00 PM. It's situated in a nice location. Three people, including the Franco-German, are already waiting outside on a bench. One Spanish guy arrives at the albergue, phones, gets the code to a box and produces a key. We get in. I unpack and have a much needed lunch, sprinkled with cerveza. I walk through the nearby park, try to visit the little fort of San Damian but it's closed. At this point I'm not sure how much staying at the albergue costs since no one has arrived yet. There are only 12 places here. I think that all of them are occupied by now.

I go into town to buy some, more, alcohol. At the entry of an Eroski supermarket I find the German with the dreadlocks laying down with his back against the wall and begging. Pumba is sitting next to him. He seems quite worthy of pity. I give him almost 2 Euros in change. He says "Wow!" From what I could notice, he didn't even have 1 Euro in coins in his begging hat. I buy a Sangria and a Gaseosa. I'm thinking that the Sangria, which doesn't come from a trusted source by me, might give me the bubonic plague again but I say to myself "what the hell...". On my way out I encounter other peregrinos at a cafe in the center of the town. I tell the Franco-German about the rastaman. Close by, a guitarist and a violinist are creating a special atmosphere embalmed in classical music. I've hummed the Hatikvah during my last days of walking so I decided to get a much better version of my humming. Turns out that the guitarist is from Russia, his ex-wife is Israeli, and the violinist is from Ukraine. The Ukrainian asked me if I'm from Norway. I did sense that they seem like foreigners before starting to talk to them. They didn't knew the Hatikvah so I had to hum it to them. They created some improvisation after my humming and also added some elements of Tarantella. After that, Verdi, a Romanian song that I hadn't recognized but seemed familiar, then some song in which the guitar started to sound like a balalaika. I enjoyed every moment of it. I tipped about 1 Euro and 5 Eurocents – what change I had in my pocket, searched my pockets and unfortunately didn't had anymore change to tip.

I wander the streets going to some places I haven't been before. I see three young student looking guys roaming the streets with their cameras and taking pics. I ask one of them if they are doing some kind of art project. Some interesting discussion ensued. I talk with them about the Camino, about Romania. The Argentinian guy, Juan, who doesn't look like an Argentinian because he is blond with blue eyes, has also been to Amsterdam. Apparently, he took a picture of one of Vermeer's descendants. Vermeer's name came up when we talked about art and told him that the painter is one of my favorites. They are working at a project themed around Design, Energy and Humanity. They have no idea about what they are doing. One of them joked and said that they should put a tent on the bridge. We head up to the albergue after wandering in the port area, talking and smoking weed. Out of an Ermita located about 100 meters from the albergue we encounter the rastaman. He is camping there and is cooking some dinner over an portable stove fueled by medicinal alcohol. He has cheap wine that comes in a box – I bought one of those boxes in Santillana. I give him what is left of the Sangria. He manages to get another donation from the students which are staying around him on the ground in a lotus position with their legs crossed. Says that he is not a pilgrim, talks smack about pilgrims "they are no real peregrinos", while doing hand gestures with imaginary walking sticks. He goes on to tell how Germany, France, Belgium, Romania are fascist countries, Spain is OK. I don't know where he is getting his facts from. Juan tells me that for his mom the visit to the Prado Museum in Madrid was one of the best days of her life. It seems like something that I would also be interested in doing. The rastaman says that he will stay an extra day in Ribadeo in order to make some money for the treatment of his dog. Pumba has worms. He tells me to leave the door open at the albergue tomorrow morning so he can come and "take some things".

Back at the albergue a Spanish girl calls the Police so that we can pay the 5 Euros accommodation fee and get our stamps. It turns out that there is no hospitalero, taking care of the albergue is the responsibility of the local Police.

Peter – said that things like the Soljenitsen Archipelago, the thought of gulags and role models like Robert Scott make him get out of the bed in the morning. While crossing the bridge he joked and said that his rational mind is saying "Jump! Jump!" but his irrational mind is saying "No, no! What are you doing?!". Funny guy.

Day 27, 17 May, Laurenza

I did about 30 kilometers today, covered plenty of hills but it didn't seemed that tiring.

Got up at 5:30 AM thinking that it's 6:30 AM. The crazy Spanish people at the albergue planned quite a lot last night, they talked about trains, touristic taxis and even questioned the policeman. I have the impression that two young guys from Germany were shamelessly smoking weed last night in front of the albergue; they knew that the policeman has to come in order to collect our staying fees. The Spanish people left at 6:00 AM, the Franco-German too.

I ate slowly, packed and left at 7:00 AM. Got to the center where I've seen yesterday a shell. I followed the shells and they led me to the port – I walked backwards on the Camino. Not good. Followed the string of shells again to some streets where the markings disappeared. I headed on a way that I thought to be an exit out of the city. I ended up at the Tourism Information Center. Unbelievable, I walked in a circle. Followed the shells again...now I see a yellow mark a few meters past yesterday's Eroski supermarket. Damn. I wasted a lot of time because I didn't noticed it the first time.

I finally managed to get out of the city. It seems that Ribadeo is a vortex just like Potes, it keeps pulling you in. A long series of hills starts after Ribadeo. While taking some pictures with interesting scenery and getting into my milk and Oreos (I like to multitask) I notice an incoming pilgrim. I thought that it's the Franco-German, thought that he also got lost. At a crossroad I take a wrong turn. I walk about 200 meters on the road above but I can't see any new mark yet. I wait. I see the peregrino coming on the little road situated downhill from my position and across a plowed field. The last sign said Limpio or something like this, I don't know why but I thought that it would lead to a garbage site (limpio – clean, I know, it's a weird deduction). I also see the Austrian couple coming on that road. Damn, three people can't be wrong and at this point and I realize that I might have taken the wrong path. I start crossing the field. It turns out that the unknown peregrino is actually an elderly woman who is now gesticulating to me and indicating that there is a ditch at the margin of the field. I try to jump over it but my leg gets caught somehow in the high vegetation and I take a fall. Fortunately, there is a lot of cushioning in the form of high grass. I would take a fall like this any time.

I start walking along with the woman and so it begins a long conversation that takes place almost all the way to Laurenza. We talk about how I got lost in Ribadeo, how in Galicia the shell signs have changed their meaning, the rays coming out of the shell point now towards Santiago, "that explains a lot" I say. We talk about the Camino and it seems that we both know Niels, about how she cracked two ribs when she fell down in Bilbao and this is why she prefers to stay at pensions and hotels because she needs extra cushioning, she doesn't want to return back home in England with the plane, it has to do with ribs, lungs and pressure, she explains. She is quite a tough woman, keeps a quick pace while climbing up the hills. Says that she is from Northern England where there are tough women. She also runs, started running at 50 and did three marathons, did some cycling, yoga, pilates, Zumba on Saturday mornings. She and her family are an active bunch.

Near a sign saying "Villar" there is a cafe where I feel that she wanted to take a break there but instead pushed on, up the hills. At this point I did about 9 kilometers "which is not bad" methinks. There are rolling hills, paths through forests, fields and little settlements. It's cloudy and cool, a good weather for walking...up hills. I'm thinking that this is a good simulation of the Camino Primitivo. It seems that the celebration of Festa das Cruces took place in some little settlement. The bins are overflowing with beer and wine bottles. There are flags of various countries posted in a firmament across a street, there is no Romanian flag. We get to an information panel and finally find out where we are: somewhere close to Vilamartin Pequeno. Not bad. Gondan is not far away, I would like to get there and call it a day. While going towards Villamartin Pequeno I can see a peregrino-looking silhouette coming towards us. It turns out to be a peregrino who went to Santiago and is now turning back to Bordeaux. I shake his hands. She has to stop because of heart palpitations, she pushed herself too much. I keep on walking after making sure that she is OK and after a few hundred meters I do a sock drying stop in a bus station fitted with a little bench and two chairs. The Austrians pass by and I offer them a chair.

Up the hills again towards Vilamartin Grande. The noise of working tractors resounds in the hills. In Vilamartin Grande I stop at a cafe where she also stopped (she got ahead of me while I was having my break). I buy some kind of chocolate cupcake for 1

Euro. A horseback group arrives. There are about 4 kilometers more to Gondan. It's early, I'm not really tired and my feet are good so I decide to continue and head to Laurenza which is 7 kilometers after Gondan. A long descent towards Gondan going through San Xue. There is no albergue there. I encounter the nomad horseback group again, "Hola cowboys!" I salute. I pass through a place called Acurva. I guess that Acurva is corresponding to O Corveiro on my sheet. The names are now in Galego which is a regional language, a mix between Spanish and Portuguese. There are only four kilometers still to go. A steep climb up through a forest starts. In her guidebook it says that's a "brief uphill climb". It didn't seemed brief at all. In the Eucalyptus forest there are raspberries on both sides of the path.

We can now see the little town of Laurenza. The stadium seems to occupy about one quarter of the town. There is a furniture manufacturing building. Getting closer, the town seems now bigger. I part ways with B., she says that it was a nice conversation. I continued going to the albergue together with the Austrians. The hospitalero comes at 19:00-19:30 PM. I rest a bit. There are not a lot of people at the albergue, there are only six pairs of boots hanging outside. I ask a newcomer, if there are any supermercados open. "No, it's a catholic celebration today, everything is closed except a bar and a restaurant". I get to a bar, get a cerveza for 1.50 Euro and a box of little chocolate cookies for another 1 Euro. I ask about Wifi, get the password and send some emails. I buy a 1906, Limited edition beer (the brand is called 1906, it's not actually made in 1906, it wouldn't probably be good if it was that old) for 1.70 Euro and some Chookies – round little things made from maize – for 1 Euro. In front of me there is a bowl of sunflower seeds so I dig in. I'm trying to get in as many calories as I can...having nothing else to eat or a place to buy food from. There are interesting, exotic looking boxes of tea with names like Mare Nostrum, Tuareg, Taj Mahal, Kalahari, Imperial Orient at the bar. They make me daydream about distant places. At 19:00 PM I get back to the albergue to pay the hospitalero, the cost is 6 Euros.

She talked about her father who went from a town in Basque country to Paris on foot, across the Pyriness Mountains because of the Civil War. Staid in Paris until the Germans invaded France. He was a brick layer so the Germans put him to work – as a prisoner of war – at the fortifications on Jersey Islands. He was only 21 years old. While in the Jersey Islands he didn't knew where exactly he is, that's why he didn't tried to escape, he might have been in the middle of the Atlantic Ocean for all he knew. The British arrived, liberated the labor camp and so he got to England. He was a socialist.

There were about 700 meters of elevation up and 600 meters of elevation down today according to the guide. Also, according to the same guidebook, tomorrow it will be a tough day with a lot of uphill going and less descending. I have no idea where I will get to tomorrow.

Day 28, 18 May, Gontan

I'm out of the albergue at 7:11 AM. I have a frugal breakfast, finishing whatever food I had left. I go to the clothes line – there are no clothes, including my socks. I'm pretty sure that I've left them overnight on the clothes line outside the albergue. Somebody must have mistaken them for their own, maybe the Austrian couple who left earlier. I search a bit through the albergue, maybe someone has taken all the clothes and put them somewhere but I couldn't find any scattered clothes. Nobody would want to steal my stinky, worn socks. There is no point getting to the bottom of this, it's time to move on, I still have pairs of socks left. About 50 meters farther after leaving the albergue there is an arrow that points to the right and up the hill which is situated behind the albergue. Walking through the forest I find two couches laid on the side of the path, between them there is a TV and a vacuum cleaner. My first thought is that maybe it's some kind of humanitarian and also promotional gesture from the local furniture company. Or who knows, maybe it was all for a good laugh. Moving that furniture required some heavy carrying up the hill.

I'm out of the woods and now I'm in the little village of Arroxo, I think. I get lost in my own thoughts and miss an obvious Camino mark. I hear someone and turn back. Another pilgrim is gesturing toward the right path. I make a mental note to be more careful. On the high hills towards my right I notice big wind mills rising even higher above the scenery. It will be an image that I will see repeatedly through most of the day. I'm not used to this kind of view.

There are dark clouds, it's windy, when I got out of the albergue it was downright chilly and I was wearing my black shorts. I take a pic of a village view with a church and a "covered" little street. Passing by the church I see a head which seemed to have been decapitated from a statue and placed in front of a window above the main entrance. "Grotesque" I think. I'm now going through fields, through tunnels of vegetation, little streets up and down again, through forests and find myself after about two hours of walking at the outskirts of Mondonedo. I pass by the Austrian couple, I salute the man with the appellative "Jägermeister" (meaning "Master Hunter" because he is wearing a green traditional hunting Austrian hat) and ask if he has only one shoe – it was hanging on his backpack – he says that the other one was at g...m..., he couldn't find the word in English. "Ah, sharing the load!" I say, "Very good" he replies. He doesn't seem to be too bright. On the way to Mondonedo - "Montevideo" from now on, why? one might ask, well, I like the name of Uruguay's capital – I take a picture that I like very much, dark and bright contrast, the sky has various shades, the green vegetation, the immaculate white of a greenhouse.

I'm thinking at all sorts of things. One of them is about how Jose Garcia, the globetrotter that I met in La Caridad, was caught and considered a spy in Syria, I don't know any more details, I read the title of an article in German from his dossier full with news clippings. He should have named himself to the Syrian authorities as Bond: "I'm Bond. Vaga Bond." Just trying to amuse myself.

Close to a Deportivo Complex I have the impression that I see a supermercado. I go downhill about 50 meters. No mercado, only a closed cafe. Damn. Up 50 steep meters I go. I would see a supermercado about 200 meters later on the right side of the road. I buy: Oreos – 1 Euro, Asturiana milk – 0.79 Euro (it gets more expensive as I go deeper into Galicia it seems), bananas – 1 Euro, jellies – 1 Euro, sliced chorizo – 1 Euro, Loran cheese – 2.45 Euros. I sit on a nearby bench to have some Oreos and milk. The Oreos have about 600 kilocalories and the milk also about 600 kilocalories, in total 1200 kilocalories which is not bad. I need all the help I can get in order to climb these hills. The Cathedral in Montevideo is huge. It towers over the whole little city which has a medieval feeling and look to it. The peregrinos sit at a cafe nearby, they left their walking sticks at the entrance. Not far after the Cathedral there is a nicely ornamented water pipe.

Outside of Montevideo starts a climb and a walk - on a nice road without gravel – on hills for the next 16 kilometers or so. On this length of the journey there are only a few small settlements, their names don't even appear on my sheet. At the entry of Maariz I notice the creative house of O Bizonte. They offer food and lodging, coffee, tea and it's donativo. Outside, there is a box with oranges and apples. A lady asks if I want coffee or tea, I say No. She says "You can take pictures, don't worry" - I was taking pictures without any worries at all. I would have liked to stay a bit but I had to go to El Baño (Spanish for toilet), which happened about two kilometers after, in the woods. There is some wood cutting going on these hills, fields, forests, small settlements. It takes forever to pass by one of those big colossal windmills which loom in the décore, they give you the feeling that you are crawling at a snails pace. Luckily, I find on the side of the road a lot of raspberry bushes with lots of berries in them. I enjoy eating and take my time even though it started raining a bit. Again, small droplets of rain. I finally get to Lousada, a location that I can find on my sheet. There are seven kilometers more to go. From Lousada, the was goes a bit down, to the right, towards the big hills with windmills and the big highway and then it goes up and up until it's on the same level with the highway. It's a steep climb and it's raining. There are some strange bunker looking type of structures throughout the forest. The road curves to the left now and away from the big highway, towards fields and scattered houses. I see a sign: Abadin – 3 km. I check my sheet. Abadin is after Gontan. Not much left to go. I see through the trees a cluster of houses which seems about one kilometer away. Gontan doesn't look that big. About 100 meters into the town, I stop at a bar which has a mini-supermarket in the back (or the mini-supermarket has a bar in the back, depends from what direction you enter the building). I buy a bread for 0.80 Euro and ask where is the albergue. "It's about 50 meters on the road and then go to the right".

Staying at the albergue costs 6 Euros and it's one

of the best, if not the best, albergue so far. It's modern, clean, big. It has anything one needs. Having access to Internet is a problem here in Galicia, you need to create an account and get a digital certificate in order to have access to Internet in albergues. The hospitalero said that it's a recent thing, it's a new system that was implemented one week ago. Said that there are bars with wifi. I eat, take a shower and rest a bit. The supermercado is in Abadin, about 500 meters away from the albergue by following the Camino route. On my way there I pass by a Loran plant, the makers of cheese. At the La Tienda shop I spend 5.83 Euros on: Fanta Limon 2 liters – 1 Euro, 1 Leche Asturiana – 0.79 Euro, 1 Salchichon Extra 85 gr. - 1 Euro, 1 chorizo Lonches Tradicional – 1 Euro, 1 bag of Batatas Fritas chips – 0.79 Euro, 1 bread – 0.80 Euro. I wanted to buy some alcohol but changed my mind, I choose junk food instead, for the calories. There is not much to do around here. It's cold, the people are walking around dressed for warmth. In Montevideo there were 13 degrees Celsius this morning.

I thought about Mordor and about the Lord Of The Rings on the journey today. I'm heading to Mordor.

Day 29, 19 May, Vilalba

Slept badly. Turned all night. Had a strange dream: I was walking some streets which had interesting walls with small openings in them; apparently, I was following someone. There is a lot of mystery in the air. Somehow, witchcraft was imminent. It was hard to hide from the person that I was following, the circular road was built in an unusual way (it's hard to explain the architecture, it's something similar to the traboules from the city of Lyon).

Someone's alarm sounds at 6:40 AM. I leave about one hour later. While getting out of Abadin I point out the correct path for one German woman what I saw yesterday at the albergue. I was cold all night long and now I have to wear waterproof gear. Soon after Abadin the road takes you through fields and forests. Even though the road is muddy and has the ever-present rocks I still prefer it to Cantabria's roads. Galicia seems to provide the best roads for walking so far. While I talk through a portion of high grass I instantly feel my left sock getting drenched. "That's not good" I think, I don't want to repeat the experience from a few days ago.

I feel in shape, well nourished from all that junk food, my feet are well, most of my fingers have a tough, hard crust of dead skin, so I begin to accelerate my walking pace. There is a lot of mist and green fields with the vegetation full of heavy dew and raindrops to cross, I can't see the scenery farther away than a few hundred meters. An encompassing white is all that I can see. I walk on roads where the canopy forms live, natural tunnels. Unfortunately, these vegetation tunnels are not enough to keep me out of the wetness, the rain permeates everything. I see the silhouette of a man who is walking slowly and who, for some reason, reminds me of the Korean guy from the first lengths of the journey; it might be his hat, his stature, his clothes, I don't know. I start thinking again at the people from the "initial group", I guess that some might have already got to Santiago, the others must be quite close. Hmm...what would happen if I would suddenly be transported 100 kilometers to Santiago? Could I meet some of them again? I pass by the man and realize that for some strange reason my initial impression proved to be correct: it is a Korean guy, but it's a new face, maybe it's John the Korean roman-catholic priest that B. told me about? I don't feel like asking, from what I know John is quite chatty and I'm in a haste, walking in the rain and wet socks proved to be my kryptonite before. I cross yet another field and yet another forest. Getting close to the main highway I see my first Santiago sign: Vilalba – 14 kilometers, Santiago – 131 kilometers. Maybe another two or two and a half hours more of walking.

I pass by the Sotomayor albergue. It doesn't appear on my sheet but it seems rustic and authentic with its rock walls and moss covered garden walls, it reminds me of the albergue near Pinares. Soon after, I find myself having to go down a steep incline so I do what I usually do in these situations: I start to run. I guess that I'm starting to adapt to the nomadic life of a backpacker: my feet are tougher now, they are covered in scales, my back muscles probably got used with the load, the backpack doesn't feel that heavy anymore after almost a month of carrying it. I am now thinking at running, at how doing the Camino can influence my running ability, at future running competitions, at my first marathon that I have yet to do. A day of carrying a heavy backpack over the hills for 30 kilometers might be tough but running a marathon seems even tougher. Running down the slope I see the Austrians: "Vamos, vamos!" enthusiastically shouts Rudy. Says that I'm fast today, "I feel in shape, my feet don't hurt anymore", "We are not in a hurry, we have time" comes the reply, "Plus, I'm trying to get out of the rain as soon as possible, if my feet are wet I will get blisters again". Fifty meters later, I find myself under a bridge. I stop to check how wet my socks and to put the footbeds back in the shoes. Strangely enough, my socks seem to be OK. The Austrians pass by me "You are an artist!", "Why?" "Your backpack is standing upright!" "Aaa" (I managed to put my backpack in an upright equilibrium, not that big deal of a trick).

In Pontebella I notice an interesting fence door with a Camino de Santiago theme on it. I hear a barking behind me, I turn back and see three peregrinos. I then pass a lonely cafe and look back again; now there are only two peregrinos. Finding refuge from the elements in a cafe-bar is not a bad idea. I pass by an enticing bus station - you know the type, the one with the small bench and flimsy walls but which at least has a roof – but say "I will pass", I already had an earlier pit stop under a bridge. More forest roads, the navigation is easy, sometimes there are forks in the road and no signs but I keep going on the "main road" without going astray on left or right side roads. That's how things work so far in Galicia. I cross bridges over springs or I just jump over springs. There is no shortage of water around these parts, that's for sure.

At some point, while passing by a farm, I find on the left side of the road a little unmanned kiosk offering for sale small bits of soft cheese – 1 Euro a piece, crepes rellenos de chocolate – 1 Euro, a "piece" of cheese about 700 grams heavy (guestimation) for 7 Euros and bits of queso semi-curado for 2 Euros. I was tented to go after the big "pieza" but after some calculations and estimations I decided that it's not worth it even though I am a fan of local, organic, farm products. On a narrow, muddy road I suddenly hear a car behind me: I get handed a flier and a map for a hostel in Vilalba. It's not the first time when I experience this, I find this to be a bad marketing method - squeezing potential clients on narrow muddy roads. This experience made me remember the guy in Cadavedo – if I remember correctly – who strolls the Camino roads in a white cheap, modest-looking car but likes to sport outside of "work" a more fancy, black, German car (Mercedes).

I get to a more urbanized area, Goiriz. Somewhere along the road I am flanked by two dogs, an hysterical German shepherd dog chained on the ride side if the road who alerted with its hystericals another, bigger, white shepherd dog which was unchained. I have to track back because I felt that squeezing between two big aggressive dogs was not a good idea; I go back and follow a street to the right which leads me to the highway. Luckily, after about 100 meters on the highway I see the Camino markings again. I notice an interesting looking cemetery with tall, pointy crosses. Soon after, I see a stork nest up on a pole. The road starts going through small settlements and fields, cutting streets again. There is a decrepit, old, abandoned house on the side of the road. I'm thinking at all the abandoned houses and properties marked with "Se vende" that I encountered so far, some of them really sparked my imagination. I guess that it's probable that some peregrino might fall in love with a house and end up buying it, thus becoming part of the Camino. I hear the buzz of an electric wire fence. Why would people employ such methods especially when they don't have much of a garden to defend? After taking some pics I manage to drop my phone – I don't get upset, it's just another test for my rugged phone, this time it ended up covered in water and sand. I'm beginning to think more and more like a Stoic and to accept all the challenges and tests that the Camino is throwing at me. All the minor or major inconveniences that I experience daily are having less and less impact on me.

Albegue de Peregrinos – 1 kilometer away. I get there at about 12:00 AM but they don't open until 13:00 PM. I spend more than one hour waiting in my sandals, trying to dry my feet, socks and shoes. My left sock got quite wet, I had to squeeze plenty of drops of water out of it. The albergue looks big and modern, it's placed between a Bombarderos fire station and a Red Cross building. "We are safe" says one of the Germans. Staying at the albergue costs 6 Euros, the wifi is working and the hospitalero seems to be from the Ambulance service.

I wait until after 16:00 PM to do some shopping because, obviously, the supermarkets are doing their siesta between 14 and 16 o'clock. Rudy the Austrian asks my name and I tell him. The Gadis supermercado is about 600-700 meters on a straight road towards Vilalba. I spend 7.68 Euros on 1.5 liters of Sangria – 1.35 Euros, Asturian milk – 0.78 Euro, Patatas chips – 0.55 Euros, 2 x Gouda Loncha – 0.90 Euro each, 2 x Chorizo Extra Loncha – 0.86 Euro each, bananas – 0.80 Euro, 250 grams of bread – 0.68 Euro. The Greip Musto juice seems to get cheaper as I go farther into Galicia. On my way back I see several peregrinos, apparently, they thought that the albergue is too far from the town so they headed, probably, towards the hostel located in the center of the city and which costs 10 Euros. The Korean guy, the older German woman to whom I gave directions and even Godfrey which I haven't seen in a few days, they all went farther. Godfrey said "I thought that you are in Santiago by now", "I had some twenty something kilometers days" I replied.

We were not that many people at the albergue...until a bunch of Spanish people and two Swedish guys appeared. A support car driver – methinks - carried a lot of luggage into the albergue, making me wonder what is going on. It turns out that the Spanish guys are doing the Camino on their bikes and that they have a support car carrying all their equipment and supplies. I get quite dizzy from the Sangria and I have a short conversation with the Catalan guy, his English not being that great. Said that Catalonia pays more to Spain than it gets in return so this would be a good motive for autonomy. It's a good motive indeed I think.

One of the German guys has the brilliant idea to dry the socks and the shoes at the hand driers in the bathroom. I abused those driers until my stuff was acceptably dry enough again.

Day 30, 20 May, Baamonde

I had a really bad sleep last night, it was hot inside the room, I was woken up at about 24:00 PM by the headlamp-wearing Spanish guys who went to bed loudly, one of them wouldn't go to sleep and stayed up while starring at his phone's screen and laughing. These noisy neighbors farted a lot in their sleep, I don't know what they were eating. The Sangria really got to me, I couldn't go to sleep after midnight, my head was spinning, my heart was beating fast and my breath fast. Other weird dreams. I wake up later than usual, pack, have some food – I didn't eat that much so I have to carry the rest. I get out at about 8:00 AM. I'm not in a hurry anyway, today there would be about 24 kilometers to do.

I go on the same road that I did yesterday when I went to the Gadis supermarket and enter the city. It seems that I haven't noticed yesterday an old machinery that looked like some kind of locomotive placed somewhere on the side of the road. Maybe it got there during the night or this morning, who knows. The arrows point me towards the center of the city. The sign has changed its meaning again but the signs embedded in the street show the correct "Galician" way. The center has plenty of old, decrepit, unoccupied buildings sprawled on small streets. The shops are also old looking and decrepit, they are closed and the streets are empty. I pass by the Vilalba tower which I saw in a regional guide back at the albergue. Seeing it in real made me think that maybe I should have visited it, if it was open of course. Nearby, there is a statue of a pregnant woman and a farmer looking fellow. She has a small doll looking thing in one hand and he has a long, thin nail, maybe a knife who knows. I guess that he is taking her to have an abortion.

I'm out of Vilalba and I find myself now on rural roads, passing by farms, pastures, going though woods. There is tall, wet grass on the road and I'm trying to avoid it as much as possible and my socks already feel wet. My socks were wet even since this morning, it seems that putting them in the fresh air and cool of the Calzados room over night did nothing. I pass by a fancy looking house with a nice looking garden. In the garden there is a huaracha with a cross on it. I haven't seen this kind of model before. Everything is green and wet. I encounter a beautiful, abandoned, little cluster of buildings. The houses are small, close to one another, there is overgrown vegetation all around, one of the houses has a small balcony, another house has a small street lamp. It seems like I have landed in a zone torn by war. I continue uphill, the path is steep and I'm not feeling to be in a good shape like I did yesterday, plus, one of my feet fingers is starting to show signs of distress. While passing through picturesque, authentic, Galician rural houses two German shepherd dogs begin barking at me. One of them is chained, the other one is unchained. It didn't seem to be an alternative way around like yesterday so I decided to stay and hold my ground if needed. The dog comes barking but his run turns to a walk. The animal approaches me, stops barking, smells and licks my hand, "You're OK" he seemed to say and gives me his stamp of approval. He keeps investigating my bag of food. A few hundred meters after, I stop in a wooded area to take care of some side business. As I am coming back I see a peregrino. I take a better look and it's B. So we meet again! We continue our discussion from where we left it a few days ago. She staid at the Panador hotel in Vilalba – lodging given to her as a gift by her son because it was her birthday, 67 years old. I tell her about the Spanish guys, she says that she saw them this morning taking breakfast at the Panador. We cross the big E-70/A-8 highway over a bridge. There is a sign on the left informing: Ribadeo – 72 kilometers, Oviedo – 212 kilometers, San Sebastian – 568 kilometers. San Sebastian...San Sebastian! That's where all of this started. A sign with this name is a weird sight for me. The distance seems long but I walked even more than 568 kilometers so far. Yes, definitely yes. I also did the Camino Lebaniego. I have come a long way and it's quite an realization for me.

B. is telling me how she might end up doing some walking through France for 2-3 days, her son and his family are having a vacation there and she wants to join them. She said that she worked with people with disabilities every summer in Santiago, last time she staid three weeks at the University where she got lodging. Told me about a picture that some Australians showed her with a big, lively snake on the road. "I saw three until now, but they were all dead". This reminded her about an incident involving her daughter in law that got bitten twice by a snake while vacationing in Scotland. She had an allergic reaction and her son was really terrified thinking that his wife might die. Remembering this unpleasant episode, B. gets melancholic, says that she would like to be by her son but that she would also like to be on the Camino. I give her some space, she is a bit tearful I think. At a cafe, the group of the - guess who? - Spanish cyclists pass by us. They are slow, it's 11:00 AM and they passed us only now. A few of them are sitting and waiting for the other to come. When they finally get together they start chatting loudly. And they chat and chat. "They are all chat and no biking" I say, "I thought that they would make it to Santiago by today, they don't carry any backpacks and they have freaking bikes".

In the settlement of Alba there is a cemetery with tall, cross-ended tombstones. There is also a German shepherd dog barking furiously at us. I can't understand his German. It seems that they prefer this race of German shepherd dogs around these parts, I've seen so many of them so far. I think about the dog that I saw in Izarbide, "El Lobo". We pass through yet another fields and settlements and at some point we encounter a house that captures our fascination and imagination. "Looks like a house where a hobbit would live in" I remark. After going on a bridge and avoiding the attack of a small yappa-type dog I see a sign: 8 kilometers to Baamonde. Not much left to go.

The road takes you through very beautiful rural fields and scenery. I don't know what exactly makes these places more special and beautiful but I enjoy them and I am delighted. Maybe it's the sun, shinning now in a cloudless blue sky, the intense green, the gardens, the lazy big dog that is sleeping in the middle of the street – maybe it's all of these things put together and even more. This scenery keeps repeating through locations like Lanelas and Casanovias. At some point a woman asks me, first in Spanish than in English with a British accent if I need water. I say no gracias and think that B. will most certainly stop to have a chat with her, they even look similar. I stop for a socks and shoes drying session in a bus station (it's always a bus station), near a sign saying Ferreira. There are about six kilometers more to go. Getting out of the bench-sized station I see a peregrino woman coming from behind. We begin to chat and the walk transforms into a dialogue again. She is a psychotherapist from Germany, has three daughters, bought hiking boots from Lidl 27 years ago. We talked about the Camino – obviously – she doesn't seem to remember locations that we've passed through like San Vincente De La Barquera or Unquera; no wonder, she just took the train through cities like Gijon, Aviles. We talked about computers, totalitarianism, about how she refused back in the 80's to take part in a census (lived in Stuttgart, now somewhere near Munchen), about the political system in Romania and Oktoberfest – she doesn't like Oktoberfest.

We arrive in an urban area. No signs, nothing. I say that Baamonde seems to be a big city according to the size of the dot on my map – it's just my impression, I haven't checked any other facts – she pulls out the ever present guide book and does a comparison with Vilalba. Baamonde looked smaller. "From what we know, we might already be in Baamonde" I say. It's about 14:36 PM and a recess bell rings at a nearby school. I tell her about the air raid sounding bells that I encountered so far in places like Ribadesella; it's a quite scary sound, you expect to see incoming airplanes any moment but then you ask yourself: "Who would attack Spain and why?!" Passing by the school I notice that Baamonde is written somewhere.

Baamonde is indeed a small town. I find the supermarket – her guide says that it's a good idea to stock up on food for the next days, apparently we will be going through a "desert". I end up buying a Musto Greip juice for 1.85 Euro (damn, the price is up again, yesterday in Vilalba was 1.35 Euro). She was looking for a sewing needle to fix her ice-breaker t-shirt. She stopped at a bar-restaurant somewhere on the right side of the main road. I continued until I got out of Baamonde. There is a hostel near a gas station but I wouldn't stay there even if you pay me; next to the gas station is a truck station with numerous trucks, no way I'm staying there in all those fumes, noise and traffic. I head back to Baamonde because it's clear by now that I missed the albergue – there is nothing for kilometers after the gas station. Back in Baamonde I ask in a bar for the location of the albergue, "it's 30 meters ahead and then to the left, near a cafe".

The albergue is not that easy to spot, you have to

pass by it really close in order to notice it. I see the Austrians staying at a table in a small garden and laughing. In the albergue I see the most beautiful hospitalera that I've seen so far, actually, one of the most beautiful girls that I've seen in Spain so far, she might be the most beautiful girl in Spain as far as I know. Staying at the albergue costs 6 Euros, there is no working Internet (it's the same internet certificate problem again – that's how I attempted to go and talk with the beautiful girl but I cowered and the discussion fizzled quickly) and it doesn't have the same facilities like the albergue before. No lavaderia and I didn't see any showers (there might be though, I haven't walked to check the whole place). It has a nice, big fireplace (which is useless now in May of course) with comfortable couches placed around it a semicircle and there is also a veranda outside where you can take a sit at a table and enjoy some fresh air. There are a lot of places here – 180 of them, it seems. Peregrinos keep arriving, it seems that the closer I get to Santiago the crowded and busier it gets. In my Dormitorio B which is a room with four beds I meet a woman who was born in Timisoara and left Romania to go to Germany some 47 years ago. She still speaks a good Romanian. My first conversation in Romanian that I have in more than a month turns out to be with a German Schwab.

I went to the supermarket again and I spent 9.62 Euros on: Oreos Banadas – 2.33 Euros, Asturiana milk to go with the Oreos – 0.88 Euro, Fanta Naranja 2l – 1.38 Euros, 2 x Mortadella 250 gr. - 1 Euro each, 1

Queso Lanchas – 2.25 Euros, 1 bread – 0.80 Euro. This time I've chosen the juice over the alcohol.

I read some magazines and learn some interesting things about the Camino while standing on one of those comfy couches in front of the fireplace.

The German woman told me that the Spanish people who do the Camino and receive their Compostela are also using it along their CV when applying for a job.

While resting at the bus station I discovered that I have thorns left in my skin around my scraped knee. I've got them when I felled down trying to jump a trench some days ago. It's curious that I haven't experienced any pain from those sharp thorns that remained embedded in me.

Day 31, 21 May, Sobrado

Today was a longer day, I started to feel that I'm getting lazy by doing twenty something kilometers days for the past days. I got to Miraz at about 10:30 AM, thought that there is plenty of time left in the day so I decided to go at least to Roxica where B. said that there should be a new albergue. In Roxica I haven't seen any albergue, it was only Casa Roxica that looked like a place where you could get some food but I doubt that since the food menu was blackened out (seen this on a billboard outside). So I went the extra mile again and ended up in Sobrado. I also thought about what B. told me about the weather forecast – it seems that it will be raining in the weekend and throughout next week all the way to Santiago and even further. I'm glad that I made the decision to make two smaller stages in one single day, meaning that I have to spend one day less in the rain. As I'm writing these lines it's pouring rain here in Sobrado. I got to the Lecer albergue just in time, a few minutes after I got in, it started pouring rain. Today it was cloudy, cold and the wind started picking up. It seems that B. was right about the forecast.

Today I've done about 40 kilometers according to my sheet and 41.3 kilometers according to a map. I'm getting closer and closer to Santiago with each kilometer. This thought encouraged me today as I kept seeing the remaining mileage to Santiago posted on pillars.

I started the day relaxed, thinking that I would do only 16 kilometers today. The Belgian headlamp bastard (yes, I shared the four beds Dormitorio B with him – again, fate is weird isn't it?) said that he will do 40 kilometers tomorrow – which is today – all the way to Sabado and that Monday he will be in Santiago and from there he will take a bus to...where? I don't know, I wasn't really paying too much attention to what he was saying. Hence, he woke up early this morning and this also made me get up early. I didn't hurried, I packed slowly and enjoyed my milk and Oreos while reading a Camino themed magazine. The Austrians, the German and the Schwab lady are already out of the albergue by the time I finish eating. I retrace my yesterday's footsteps until the exit out of Baamonde and beyond. The route seems to be on the N-VI highway.

On today's first kilometers on the highway I could see from time to time a group of people ahead of me, maybe some minutes away. A convoy of 4x4's passes on the highway hurrying to who knows what. The Camino crosses the train tracks and finally enters a forest, ruta "Das Bidueiras". The Camino passes by the Capela San Alberte and continues on one of the most beautiful paths that I've seen so far. It's a peaceful little road with soft ground, there is green in all directions, moss on the low walls that border the road, there are lots of prehistoric looking ferns. It looks like an ancient road. It made me think at Visigoths, Moors, the Reconquista. I wondered if any Moor ever got up to this place. Out of this magical place which is maybe only one kilometer long, starts a series of small settlements. At the first house there are lots of dogs, two or three of them are chained but there are other three smaller yappa-type of dogs who are not. They barked at me, obviously, and got quite close. I could hear some laughter coming from inside the house; well, at least somebody was finding the vicious hell raising little dogs funny, I didn't.

Taar, Bondoncel, Digane. Again, there are some German shepherd dogs that roam freely on the streets but they don't seem to be aggressive. Somewhere after these small settlements there is a cafe, Apoyo Al Peregrino, 400 meters away – says the sign. I guess that the group ahead of me must have disappeared somewhere in a cafe like this since I haven't seen them all day. In a settlement, about ten minutes before Miraz there is the house of the sculptor Francisco Javier Lopez "Chacon". I didn't knew about this place, I was passing by and heard the nice latino music and then I saw the Australian guy that passed me about one kilometer before, in the garden talking to a man. I ask: "What is this place? I thought that it's an albergue." "We can get a stamp here" comes the reply. I get my stamp on my peregrino passport and it looked cool: the sculptor melted red wax with a torch and then he applied a sigillum with a Templar looking cross on it. It's the best stamp that I got so far! I visit his one room museum and notice all the little sculptures with crosses on them, a bear's hide, some Aztec themed things, his little panoply of arms, "La espada e original?" "No, only the Vietnamese machete and a bayonet from a Mauser are original". Given the Aztec themed items I ask him if he went to Mexico, Javier says no and points with one finger to the ground. I see some Australian-looking hats, "Australia?" "No..." says with a mimic and intonation that leak the unspoken fact that he stayed in Spain all his life. He says about my bottle of Fanta that is "No Bueno...Vino!" I give him a small three Euros donation – placed the coins on the head of the horned sculptured demon-looking creature in the garden. I feel grateful for the awesome stamp and that he allowed us in his little but interesting musem.

The albergue situated at the entry of Miraz is a private one, alojamiento is 10 Euros, a menu is 8 Euros. The municipal one is a bit farther on a road that splits from the Camino. Between Miraz and Roxica there is a portion of the road that is maybe one kilometer long and it's the most beautiful portion that I've seen so far. The road is very similar to a mountain trek through the forest, bouldery steps, you feel like you are in a true wilderness, you can see the landscape for kilometers all around you and it's all hills and forests. Unfortunately, my enthusiasm is soon curved by the fact that I'm walking on a road made for cars again. Up to Roxica and beyond, this road takes you through serpentines up, down and around hills, through woods and fields. I stop to take a break and sit on a bus station bench, I dry my stuff and eat some food. A German looking couple and the Australian pass by me. I would catch them later.

In the little village of Marcela I notice an interesting collection of aviary specimens in a garden: screaming peacocks, hens and turkeys. After Marcela the road starts going downhill in a slight but sure angle. I follow the Australian who is limping - he has a bad knee – through an Australian looking landscape with white sandy limestone, eucalyptus trees, it's bright, sunny and warm. I pass him and try to encourage him by saying "There are only about seven kilometers left, maybe an hour and a half more of walking, we are close", "I like your enthusiasm". He seemed to be struggling. About one kilometer later I see a sign informing that there are eight kilometers more to Sobrado.

I walk and then run – it's downhill, so in most cases I do this – for a few kilometers on the highway until the Camino steers me to the right and through some urban settlements and from there back in the forest. While walking through the forest I get caught up in my own thoughts, I "wake" up and ask myself if I'm still on the right path. I still am. There are dark clouds, the wind is starting to blow harder. I'm in Igr...? now, I check and it's not even on my sheet but after my estimations I must be close to Sobrado. Maybe thirty more minutes of walking left. I came upon a lake and I remember seeing a picture of it in one of those magazines that I read in Baamonde, the picture in the magazine looked much more picturesque, in reality the lake isn't that much of a big deal, it reminds me of Lake Ciric back at home. I pass the lake and I'm finally in Sobrado. At some point, after a few hundred meters in, I lose track of the arrows. I see the big monastery and I'm heading towards it. I see a "hecer albergue" sign again so that means that the albergue must be somewhere close. It's starting to trickle and I realize that I don't have much time until the real rain will come.

I get to the (private) albergue which costs 10 Euros. I don't wait around too much and ask about the supermercado. "About 100 meters down the road, after the plaza, to the right. There are two of them." I get to the one on the right side on the road – haven't seen the other one – and I spend 5.90 Euros at the Onda supermarket: 2 liters of Fanta Limon – 1.25 Euros, Queso Lonchas – 1 Euro, Pechuga de Pavo – 1 Euro, Twins (a replacement for Oreos) – 1 Euro, Leyma milk – 0.75 Euro, bread – 0.90 Euro. I run through the pouring rain and get back at the albergue. Here, there are three other people, the limping Korean old man, the German lady who didn't wanted to stay at the albergue outside of Vilalba and another German lady. I do some Googling and learn some new stuff about Spain. I realize that tomorrow it will be Sunday so in Arzua there will be nothing open. I ask the hospitalero if there might be something open tomorrow in Arzua, he doesn't knows. I go again at Onda and spend 3.95 Euros on: sliced bread – 1 Euro, Queso Lonchas – 1 Euro, Pechuga de Pavo from Bonnatur – 1 Euro, cerveza Aurum – 0.95 Euro. I have to run through the rain again. The beer isn't that great.

While staying on that bench in the tiny bus station I found out what those cisterns that I've seen numerous times and that are towed by tractors really contain: natural fertilizers.

Day 32, 22 May, Arzua

It's more than a month now since I have started this journey.

I woke up later than usual, at 7:20 AM. After eating my "Twins", drinking my morning milk, packing and going to the loo, I am out of the albergue about one hour later. The German lady tells me that she will not be heading to Arzua today, she will do only 11 kilometers, there is an albergue in Boimorto. She didn't seemed to be in a good shape yesterday. There is no hurry to finish the Camino anyway. Some are doing it in stages, some are going back home on foot, some end up staying in Santiago and volunteering, some are even going farther to places like Morocco. There are no rules.

I started the day being convinced that today would be just another 20 kilometers day, which is not such a difficult task. As soon as I get out of the town and start climbing the first hill of the day with all of yesterday's shopping in my backpack and also a bottle half full of Fanta on top of my backpack I'm starting to sense the opposite. For some reason, when I look back in hindsight I have the tendency to minimize the effort that it took me in order to achieve something. Even in those shorter distance days I've put in a lot of work, sweat, blood and tears.

I'm following two pilgrims that I haven't seen before up the hill. We walked in a "convoy" with a distance of about 10 meters between each of us. I take a short piss break and lose distance on them. It's cold and my nose is running, I have to blow air through my lips so that the watery mucus doesn't end up in my one month old mustache and beard. The sky is a mix between dark and light. The sun is struggling to brightly shine through the dark clouds. I pass through a small settlement with fancy houses called Casanova. At the exit of this small settlement there is Casa Casanova, number one. The road alternates between quiet, beautiful forests and small settlements with houses that have the ever present barking dogs. On such a forest road, maybe one kilometer or more long, my mind forgets about the Camino, about roads, about signs, about my aching back and sore feet. What awaits me after the Camino? I don't feel that I want to return to my former life. The forest road takes a turn to the left, towards the highway. A sign: the Boimorto albergue is 3000 meters away. Some kilometers farther down the highway I pass by the albergue, not by passing first an interesting shop with old, classic motorcycles and an old car on display, in the settlement of Corredoiras. At some cafe in Boimil, the old Korean guy and one of those two new pilgrims that I've seen this morning are enjoying a break.

Arzua is now 12 kilometers away, Boimorto is 3 kilometers away. Boimorto is a bigger town than I expected, it has a mini-supermarket somewhere at the entrance to the city. The mini-supermarket (mini-market?) is open which made me question my yesterday's plan of stocking up. In front of the shop there is a family that are buying and carrying canisters of gas to the car like there is no tomorrow. On this portion of the Camino the markings are quite bad, a sign appears sporadically every now and then, an arrow or a pillar, you don't know what to expect. I notice a lot of small cars the kind of which I haven't seen before; I find a parked one and the brand is Microcar, I will have to look up of this brand later on. I get duped by a bad pillar sign, I think that I should have take it to the left at the point where there is a sign informing that there are 10 kilometers to Arzua. Instead, I continued on the same street until it led me out of the town and into the forest. In front of me I can see another pilgrim some 100 meters ahead stopping at a crossroad, he checks his guide or maybe a map, looks behind and then continues straight ahead. Given the fact that his has a guide or a map I assume that he knows what he is doing so I follow him. I enter the forest for a little "break". I hear some barking in the distance to my left, and I expect a dog to come from nowhere but I see a little hopping deer instead. So there are deers in Spain after all! All of those deer related signs are not put for nothing it seems. I also get to that crossroad. There are no Camino marks, no nothing, so I continue on, walking straight ahead. Two cyclists pass by me, I pass by a stadium, a police car comes from the opposite side of the road – I take all these as "reassuring signs" that I'm on the right track. I continue for a little while until I get to another crossroad. There are no Camino marks, no nothing. There are four possible routes that I could go on from this point, just like the last crossroad. I'm starting to think at this point that I got lost. I get my sheet and check the name Sendelle – which I've seen at the crossroad - against it. The name Sendelle appears on my sheet indeed! From Sendelle to Arzua there are about eight kilometers. I take a turn to the left, downhill towards Sendelle and hoping to encounter the Camino again, if that doesn't happen I will just follow the highway straight to Arzua.

I thought that this would be an easy day but I just got lost and had to take a detour. I keep seeing Vedado De Caza signs on the side of the road. The Catalan guy told me back in Vilalba that Caza means hunting. I'll have to check for myself what this really means. I hope that I'm not on hunting grounds though. I go through the little settlement of Saamil and get to a crossroad again; I finally see the Camino pillar again and two pilgrims slowly coming on the Camino towards my direction. Sendelle is not far and there I make a stop on a stone bench in front of the Santa Maria de Sendelle church. The sun is burning hot between heavy dark clouds carried by a strong wind. It's a good occasion to consume some of the stuff that I'm carrying, it's better to have them in me rather than on me. And to dry my shoes and socks. My "waterproof" trekking shoes are no match for the wet grass from the forest. Not far from the church there is a blueish building built in 1940. It made me think that while in some parts of the world there was war and destruction, nice little houses like this one were being built here.

The Camino continues through rural settlements and fields. There are six kilometers more to Arzua. I was very cold after I left my resting spot on the stone bench and it even rained for a little while but now I'm getting more and more warm and the sun is showing up between clouds more frequent. A road sign cow says "Buen Camino!". It made me think about the other funny signs that I've seen so far. In O Castro I observe S-shaped lines in the plowed ground with green little spruces in them. From O Castro there is a long, straight line leading uphill to Arzua. The Camino pillars disappear again at some point, only a few, barely distinguishable arrows drawn on the ground can be noticed. In the Val de Jso I notice a tent in an area shaded by a group of trees. Speaking of trees, these places would have been only fields if it wouldn't have been a concerted effort to plant trees.

I go up the hill and something that seems like an urban area pops up. A stadium, a market with all kinds of people in it, Koreans, who give the place a very exotic feeling, other pilgrims, Gipsy looking people, Arab looking people, mulattoes and so on. For somebody who spent most of his last days walking through sparsely populated areas, this bazaar and this amalgam of different people is a very interesting site to see. The albergue is 200 meters away.

I check in at the Casa Del Peregrino for 10 Euros. I discover a bit later that the municipal albergue is just meters away on the other side of the street – it had a large crowd in front of it and I assumed that it's a bar or something like that and I also tend to avoid large crowds so it's no wonder that I didn't spotted the albergue. There are only three other people here, me included, and including the German lady that I keep encountering in albergues and that changed her mind about doing only 11 kilometers today. There are not bad conditions here at the albergue, it's quiet, it has wifi and I use it to plan my next moves after Santiago, maybe I will go to Porto by bus and stay there for a day after doing Santiago-Muxia-Finisterre-Santiago. I ask for a supermercado, the hospitalera says that there is a little one which is open and it's located somewhere on a road right to the plaza. I wonder around and can't find it so I end up going to the restaurant-bar near the plaza. I overpay there 6.90 Euros for a simple hamburger, a small slice of almond pie and a Desperados cerveza. There are plenty of pilgrims that are floating around now that the Camino Frances and the Camino Del Norte met together in Arzua, it's like the two tributaries of the Nile – the White Nile and the Blue Nile - that meet near Khartoum to form the great Nile. As a "Northerner" I am not used with the presence of so many other pilgrims. I imagine that Santiago will be packed. We all go on the same roads, more or less, but we experience them in so many and unique, personal ways.

Music is one of the things that I've missed so much in this Camino. I often thought at various songs, tried to remember the lyrics and to hum them.

I went to the Mandala cafe afterwards and spent 4.5 Euros worth of heavy coins on a 1.5 Euros glass of beer and a 3 Euros dessert invented by the husband of the lady servicing the place. The Mandala dessert consisted of a yogurt looking thing drowned in a crème brûlée syrup. It was definitely good and it was worth the money spent. The German lady and a new woman acquaintance of her tried it first and they were quite pleased so I also decided to try it out of curiosity. The place is decorated with prayer flags, Buddha statues, a bell that is imprinted with Titanic 1912 and that ends up with a pony pulley. There are also pictures of Mandalas and some foreign currency banknotes with Mao Zedong and Gandhi on them. The lady was three years ago in Nepal and went together with her husband, climbed on Everest up to 3000 meters in November. Said that the weather was good while the sun was up, when the sun came down the cold made its presence. Pretty much like on the Camino.

Day 33, 23 May, Pedrouzo

I started the day relaxed, thinking that I will do only about 20 kilometers today. The other guy in the room got up early which also made me get up early.

However, I preferred to stay a bit longer in bed and to use the Internet. I have a frugal breakfast and from the window of the kitchen I could see a procession of people going on the Camino. I wondered where all these pilgrims were coming from since from what I knew there were no albergues in that direction. I am out of the albergue at 8:00 AM and I soon join the procession. It is something new to me, to have so many pilgrims on the Camino. If I were to pick up a stone and throw it in front of me or behind me there would be a good chance that the rock might hit somebody.

The Camino takes me downhill and then uphill again, through a forest and on a hill from where you can see Arzua in distance and even farther than it, areas covered in a morning fog. My thoughts are concentrated on the new reality of the Camino. Just when you think that you figured out the Camino it comes back to throw at you another twist. The pilgrims from the Camino Frances look different from what I'm used to see. The two in front of me, an elderly man and a elderly woman are two examples. The man has a small, school-sized backpack and is wearing a set of big headphones, he takes selfies of himself. The woman is wearing a black kerchief, pajama looking pants and is sporting a small backpack. Passing her I also notice that she wears makeup and lipstick. I would see her again throughout the day, sprinting – this time without the man, who was left behind – and braking branches from small trees and putting them on her back, without even stopping. She even manages to add a long, beautiful white flower to her collection. It made me laugh each time I saw the woman in action. Such a bizarre person, maybe a weekend peregrino, who knows. And who knows why she is breaking and carrying all those branches and flowers. The Camino Frances people seem zombie like, walking slowly in a long procession. They usually have small backpacks like they are going in a one day hike. I pass by a bunch of them.

The Camino takes you through beautiful and scenic woods, little settlements with neat gardens. On bins there are writings like: 2016 – The year when we end our ignorance, or something like that. I have no idea what they are referring to, I guess that I'm an ignorant, I must admit. The wall of wisdom doesn't offer you wisdom or answers, it offers only existential and religious questions. At the first cafe I notice the Korean guy getting up from his chair and starting to walk slowly with his usual limp. He must have woke up early and left early but he got only to this point. Among all of these people you are not alone but you are alone, you are alone but not alone with your thoughts. I catch up with him and engage him in conversation. By this time I was thinking of going all the way to Santiago, but what the hell, I can take some time to speak with him. It turns out that he is a globetrotter, spends one or two months every year traveling and in this way he managed to visit more than 100 countries. He went through Bulgaria, Romania (Bucuresti, Brasov, Bran, Sinaia, Peles), Hungary. This is his third Camino and he went through Spain and Portugal some 20 years ago too. I asked if he was in Nepal and he replied that "it's a tourist country". I tell him about my ambition of climbing the top of the highest mountain on every continent, including Everest. Said that I should check out the mountains in Taiwan – it turns out that he is from Taiwan not Korea – they are almost 4000 meters tall. Said that a lot of Koreans are Catholic and that they are doing the Camino for religious purposes. I ask him if he went to Korea, "Yes, about three hours flight from Taipei, not a long distance". Said about North Korea and Cuba that are special places, he went to Cuba, "a nice, peaceful, relaxed place with good music". He stops to take a picture of a bin which has the lyrics of the Beatles song written on it: "Only if all the people...".

I'm now in Salceda, there are only 27 kilometers more to go. He is struggling uphill so I have to leave him behind – he wants to get today to a place only 10 kilometers from Santiago so he can do them tomorrow and catch the 10:00 Mesa at the Cathedral. I start passing by hoards of pilgrims. There are plenty of albergues offering alojamiento along the way and now, some kilometers after Arzua, plenty of cafes, bars offering menu del dia, tapas, bochadillos, coffee and so on – for the hungry and thirsty pilgrim. There are no supermercados or even mini ones, of course.

The clouds give way to the sun after a cold morning. The clear sky is now criss-crossed by white trails left by the fleeting airplanes. Must be all those pilgrims going back home from Santiago. Speaking of going back home, I also see a few pilgrims making the way back from Santiago and towards, who knows what destinations. I have no idea through what locations I'm going because of the lack of signs and the way that the

Camino cuts straight through settlements sometimes, but what I do know is the distances, which are marked on the Camino pillars, and I'm checking the distances against the ones on my sheet. I see a ship on a gate and it reminds me of the Galleon at the albergue in San Vincente. I'm starting to realize that by now there are not a lot of things left to be discovered but only old things to be reminded of.

Today would be the day to observe and to learn more about these strange "Southern" pilgrims. A graffiti at the entry of an underbridge passage says S. Irene. I check it out on my sheet – 22 kilometers more to go. There is a municipal albergue in S. Irene but nobody seemed to have stopped there. After S. Irene the path goes through a forest. For some reason, the group in front of me prefer to go on the highway instead. On the short, maybe 200 meters long path through the forest I am finally alone, there are no others in front or behind me. This would change as soon as I make haste to Pedrouzo. I'm feeling hungry by now, I haven't eaten properly for a while now. I still have 500 grams of sliced bread that I'm carrying, I guess that should do it, if necessary, until Santiago. At a crossroad I notice that some people are choosing to go again on the highway rather than on the Camino path. The Camino takes you somewhere through a field and the woods, the highway takes you to an urban area. I decide to follow them and I soon find out the name of the area: Pedrouzo. I pass by the municipal albergue and about 10 meters farther I get to a mini-supermarket. I spend there 4.5 Euros on: Locan cheese, sliced chorizo and a 1 liter Martens bottle of beer. I sit at the table in front of the store, eating and thinking about what to do next. I decide that I want to avoid staying in Santiago too much, I don't like crowded places and groups of other pilgrims especially the ones sitting at cafes. Tomorrow I would do about 40 kilometers to Negreira and just pass through Santiago.

I wait about 15 minutes until 13:00 PM for the albergue to open. Cost: 6 Euros. I go afterwards back to the store where I spend 5.40 Euros on: Twins, milk, sliced chorizo, one bottle of vino and a table cloth with the map of Galicia and the Galician flag to give as a gift when I will get back home.

I ask the girl that keeps standing on the front patio of the albergue why is she doing that. She has an inflammation of the feet so she took a taxi and is now waiting for her group to arrive. They started in Boimorte. Turns out that she also does the Camino Del Norte, she is also a runner, read Born To Run, bought Vibram Five Finger shoes after reading it. She did the though GR-20 trek in Corsica in 10 days. Also goes to Porto and then to Montpellier and to a little medieval looking town close to it to work in a shop in order to help a friend. She is from France. Says that Lisbon is a beautiful place, cheap and with friendly people.

I went to another store where I bought sliced chorizo, queso semimadura, 1 liter of beer, 125 grams of a mix of seeds, nuts dried corn, and a little box of jellies for about 6 Euros in total. This was after consuming the whole bottle of Lagano or Lagada Galego wine. The fruity white wine was good...and cheap. It had a bit of sparkle in it. I begin drinking the beer and eating the mix. That Almond tart, Tartas Ancano, that I've seen earlier just keeps coming up in my mind. Yesterday I paid 2.50 Euros for a little slice, now I can have it all for 7 Euros. The tart it's quite big though, 700 grams and 100 grams has 500 kilocalories. I will declare today to be the day of excesses so I just go again to the shop "next door" and buy it. I want to speak again to the French girl so I wait on one of the benches outside the albergue. She went together with her group to have dinner. I munch on that tart and even offer a slice to one of the Poles – who had a lengthy conversation with an Argentinian girl – and drink the beer. And I wait. When she comes back I offer her some of my tart but she says that she is full and doesn't stay around.

At about 2:00 AM I go to the bathroom to have a pee. I end up throwing up three times, each time time a big volume, fact that astonishes me. I wonder how could I have puked all of this matter...but 2 litters of beer, 1 liter of wine, not eating much for the day and then eating about ¾ of a big tart rich in calories should do the trick. I make quite a mess in the toilet. Someone came in the bathroom shortly, seconds, after I puked and most probably heard what was going on. I felt better afterwards and could go to sleep.

Day 34, 24 May, Santiago De Compostela

I wake up early, shortly after 6:00 AM. There are

some early risers. I didn't stay around for too much, I wanted somehow to make up for yesterday's excesses. I make multiple runs between the dormitorio which is upstairs and the dinning room which is downstairs in order to bring all my stuff. I eat the Twins and drink my milk. I forget about the tart and I'm reminded about it when I'm packing. I decided to just leave it on the table. Good riddance because now I'm associating it with a bad experience. I'm out of the albergue and it's early. I'm starting to follow the peregrinos in front of me because I have no idea where the arrows and the Camino is. Maybe they know or see something that I don't.

Out of the little city and now in a dark forest. It's the rainy season again. It's so dark in the forest that I'm thinking of getting my headlamp and to start wearing it but it's too much of a hustle to get my backpack down, to unpack and then to pack and lift the backpack again. Thinking about it, I never actually used my headlamp, I only used my little pocket light once in Ribadeo if I remember correctly. I brought the headlamp with me because I was hoping to use it in order to explore a cave but the places that have caves - Camino Lebaniego and Ribadesella - are now far away.

The Camino takes us through quite a lot of forest this morning. After the first cafe encountered today and which already has a few pilgrims in it, a steep climb up the hill starts. I have a short conversation with an Italian guy who is sporting a flag on his backpack. I thought that it's the flag of Sicily and asked him if it is, he says no, it's Sardinia and that the flag of Sardinia is similar to the flag of Corsica, "Corsica, one black man, Sardinia, four black men". I don't know why the two islands have black men on their flags. He asks me where I'm from and I say that I'm from Romania. Says that he was in Romania before, rented a car and visited Transylvania, Brasov, Timisoara, Baile Herculane. He stops for a break – did I mentioned the fact that the hill is really steep? - so I leave him behind and I pass by other pilgrims up the hill. The rain starts to catch up so I have to put my rain gear on. It's now raining heavily and without those tiny, small droplets. I'm on top of the hill and there is a sign that says that there are 12.5 kilometers to Santiago. The path is close to the airport and the sound of planes taking off is very loud. I can hear them but I cannot see them because of the wall made of trees.

The path goes downhill and takes you only meters away from the airport's fences. There is a sculpture with a shell and Santiago. A peregrino on bike passes by me but stops when faced with a steep uphill climb, he dismounts and starts pushing his bike. I go through a short but beautiful portion of the Camino with lush green vegetation, moss everywhere and converging streams. All the lush green and the moss makes me think that rain is common around these parts. It's a slight incline until the next point with bars and cafes on the side of the road with several pilgrims inside that are trying to escape the rain. From there on, there is a steady up climb, usually in steep episodes after "breaks" - flatter sides in urban areas – all the way up to Mount Gozo.

I keep up with a fast walking girl who jokingly

says to other peregrinos "all the rain was kept for the last part to Santiago". She must have been on the Camino Frances, methinks. I noticed that the Camino Frances people are well tanned, I guess that they had good weather most of the time. I keep the pace with her going uphill and at some point I start a conversation with her by saying "it's a good day to walk"- I heard her saying "mierda" about the weather at some previous point. Yes, I stole the "it's a good day to walk" expression from Peter. Turns out that she is from Los Angels but grew up in San Francisco, her name is Gabi short for Gabriella, she traveled through Europe for the past two months, started the Camino two weeks and a half ago, goes back to the States for her graduation ceremony (UCLA), wants to specialize in coffee and the politics around coffee, "very interesting" I say because it really is interesting for me, I don't drink coffee at all so it's a new undiscovered world for me. I speak to her a bit in Romanian. She says that she is poor so that she walks back home everywhere, at a fast pace; she can't run because she torn the ligaments in her knee. She is traveling with a group so she stops at some point and says that she will wait for her group. Maybe it was my joke about her in which I said that she is a Mexican drug dealer after she said that she promotes coffee drinking with coffee being a "legal drug". We had a nice conversation though. She says bye and that she will see me again in Santiago.

There is a sign with Monte Gozo. I thought that I was already on Monte Gozo or even passed it given all the uphill climbing, but no, the Mount was just beginning. After the sign there is yet another steep portion. There is a fence on the left side of the road and in the fence are jammed crosses made out of sticks. I get my first view of Santiago. A group of three bikers is going uphill and they are victoriously chanting and making all kinds of ecstatic noises, "Santiago!". A bit of their enthusiasm rubs off to me. In the urban part of Mount Gozo there are various albergues that advertise their services. A man in a strange, minimalist vehicle slowly makes his way down the hill. He is nonchalantly carrying an umbrella in one hand. After the monument on top of Mount Gozo the road finally goes downhill towards Santiago. I run down the steep road. Some hundreds of meters after, I start following the procession of strange looking pilgrims with their rain capes, in various colors and shapes. I see the first Santiago city sign and a map of Santiago.

I'm finally in Mordor! I slowly advance towards the center of the city, through rain and through intersections. I see some albergues advertising their stuff again and I wonder if I should get an accommodation. Neah, I should get to the center of the city first, to the Cathedral, maybe there are albergues around it as well. I lose track of the arrows at some point but I manage to see the top of the Cathedral from a high point and wander through the streets towards it. There are a lot of people in the streets, a lot of locals, tourists and pilgrims. This makes me feel like in Gijon again. Now I'm thinking that it might not be that easy to get accommodation. I see various buildings, take pics and get to a place where a large group of Asian people are taking a group photo. Hmm...it seems to be the Cathedral but I'm not sure. The angle, a part of the building is in renovation, it doesn't look like the mental image that I had about it. I have seen the Cathedral and symbols of it many times along the Camino. There is a security guard at an entry and a "No mochillas" sign. I have to find an albergue since I cannot enter in the Cathedral with my backpack.

I wander the streets a bit further and I come across a Peregrino Welcome Center. There are people inside. It seems that you can get your Compostela from here. I had no idea about this, I thought that I will get the Compostela from the Cathedral. I get out of the rain and wait in line about an hour to get my Compostela. Turns out that I'm sitting behind the group which the French girl is traveling with. Turns out that she is also there but somewhere in front of the line. I guess that she took the taxi again, I never saw her on the road. I try to ignore her but she says hello. I overheard a conversation in French earlier between another French lady in the group and somebody else. Apparently, if I understood correctly, she will not go to Finisterre and Porto, instead, she will take a flight straight to Montpellier.

After getting the Compostela, I wander the streets looking for alojamiento. I have no idea where I'm heading, the public maps located in various parts of the city are of no good. I have to get to the Tourism Information Center. I pass by the Cathedral again, a lady accosts me and asks if I need a place to stay, I say no, a few meters later, another old lady asks me the same thing. What the hell, I'm tired of the situation of being in search mode and carrying a backpack which is now heavier given all of yesterday's shopping. She guides me through the streets to the place, "it's a few minutes away" she says, costs 15 Euros, individual room, she asks me if I'm German, "No, I'm Romanian", "Ah, Romanians are good people" she says. We pass by a hostel, I stop and I'm trying to explain to her that I want to go and check it out "Ver". She doesn't seem too happy about it so she leaves. The hostel door is locked, there are people with luggage inside. I guess that it's fully booked or something like that so I keep searching for another place. I wander around again for a long time. I finally find the Tourism Information Center. There, a very helpful lady phones a hostel with a name starting with M..., it's fully booked, she then calls at the Last Stamp hostel, there are two places free and she makes a reservation on the name Stefan. I use the map that she gave me to find the hostel. When I get there I realize that it's the same hostel that I tried to get into earlier. Damn! Some streets earlier I noticed a girl that was wondering the streets just like me, she is ahead of me and it turns out that we are looking for the same place. She gets to the hostel just seconds ahead me. Damn! I wonder if there are still places left, I can see that there are tourists inside, waiting in the reception area. I can't believe all the mistakes that I'm making. Now I will, most probably, have to start searching for a new location again, I'm pretty sure that the receptionist will say that there are no more places left. I anxiously wait in line and when my turn comes I say to the receptionist that there is a reservation on my name. It turns out that my reservation is still good and I manage to get a bed for 18 Euros.

I unpack and go to the kitchen area to eat something. I notice there a familiar face going into the little room adjacent to the kitchen area and which has a place for clothes drying, a table, some nice chairs and a little cozy couch. The room has a glass door, a glass wall and a glass ceiling and it's situated in a little courtyard so there is a lot of natural light inside. I remember who the familiar face is, it's the German from San Vincente De La Barquera. He doesn't know who I am initially. He tells me that Juliana got somewhere near Aviles and then she had to leave for Germany; she had feet problems, he told me about the German woman and her daughter, Guldrun? and Gerda? (didn't got their names right). They were yesterday around Santiago and left for a 2-3 days "holiday" in the little town of Cee, located somewhere on the Camino Finisterre. He showed me pics with other people but I couldn't recognize anybody else. Gerold, because this is his name, did the Camino Frances and the Camino Del Norte now, he did the Camino Finistere the first time so he won't be doing it this time. He did the Inca Trail, said that there is a limit of 500 persons per day on it, you need some kind of application for a permit months in advance. He wants to do the Kilimanjaro and I tell him about my Seven Summits plan. He tells me about the differences between the Frances and the Del Norte. I give Gerold my email address.

I go out to wander the streets again searching for the Tourism Information Center for Galicia (yes, there are two distinct centers, one for the region of Galicia and one for the city of Santiago) to get a map and some information about the road to Finisterre. I encounter a Froiz supermarket on the way there and end up spending 5.88 Euros on: Chorizo 2 in 1 offer – 1.45 Euros, 200 gr. of cheese for 1 Euro, Oreos - 1.59 Euros, Asturiana milk – 0.75 Euro, Don Simon Mango and Apple juice – 1.09 Euros. I was tempted to get a Desperados cerveza at 1 Euro.

The rain started pouring again making my street wandering wet. With a map in one hand and a bag in the other I make my way to the other Tourism Information Center where I get all the information I need. At the previous one I was the only Romanian guy who went there – they ask you where are you from and then they register your response, for statistic purposes I guess. On my way back I stop at a souvenir shop and spend almost 3 Euros on a postcard and a little glass cup for shots that has a Spanish theme on it: Flamenco dancers, it should make for a nice gift for Claudiu (my friend in Portugal).

The plaza is impressive, you feel so small standing there.

Gabi backpacked from Mexico to Peru. Quite impressive.

I spent some really special moments alone in the "outside" glass room, drops of rain splashing on the transparent roof, a bit of classic opera music coming from the kitchen area.

Day 35, 25 May, Negreira

Milk and Oreos for breakfast, it started to be a tradition by now. I am out by 8:20 AM. I use the map that I received yesterday to navigate myself out of Santiago. In a bar close to the albergue I have the impression that I see someone familiar, someone who has a specific limp. I go inside the bar and it turns out that it's indeed the Taiwanese guy. He says that he will take a bus to Lisbon. I say that I will go to Finisterre. I say goodbye and leave. "It was nice knowing you!" Soon enough, a pilgrim procession forms again as I catch up with the people that are ahead of me.

The Camino goes through a small park, then downhill and then we are back in rural country. From the point where a little spring passes there is a new ascent to be made. On the path somewhere to the right there is a tent, in front of it a pair of boots, a towel and a t-shirt on a clothes line and a little can prompting for donations. The whole setting seems fake to me. I put my rain gear on because the weather is getting shifty again, dark clouds and short showers. Soon, the occasional showers will transform in a torrential rain that will last a few hours. I start digging into my jellies.

I'm in good spirits, I achieved my mission yesterday and from now on it's a bonus for me. I'm thinking and reminiscing at various moments that happened in the last 30 days and more. We get up on a hill and on the other side there is Santiago and its Cathedral seems to dominate the city. The path takes a left turn and I have the impression for a moment that we are heading towards Santiago again. Instead, we go through the woods. I'm carrying extra food in my backpack again and I also have a bag with the jellies and the rest of what is left of the milk inside. I'm not feeling in shape, I'm feeling rather sluggish. It took me some effort to do my backpack this morning. I pass through settlements and have no idea about their names. We get to the settlement of Aguapesada. In distance and in front of us there is a high barrier consisting of forested hills. My first thought is that it seems that the Camino is taking us straight to it and then we will have to go over it. This will be a daunting task. The road goes in a long, straight path downwards and then makes a left. The rain stops for a bit and the sun manages to throw a few rays through the clouds. I profit from this ephemeral moment, knowing that it wont last long, to sit on a bench and finish drinking my milk and to eat some more jellies. I read on a paper that I got from the tourism center that apparently, there is a Puente Medieval somewhere around these parts. I guess that the Puente Medieval is the one that is on front of me now. I take a better look, hmm...I'm not sure if it's medieval. I get passed by the group that traveled with the French girl. She is not with the group, maybe she is behind or she just left.

A steep uphill climb starts after Aguapesada. Walkers and bikers stumble sluggishly and progress slowly on the steep slopes. Once I get up on the hill I take a drying break on a bus station bench outside of Castineiro. My socks are wet, I have to squeeze droplets of muddy water out of them, I beat my socks against the pillars of the bus station. It's time to change my socks even though my spare ones are not actually dry. I carry on, catching up with some of the folks. I see an eclectic looking group of youngsters coming out of a cafe – they will be my vanguard for a good few kilometers until some point close to Negreira. Three boys – a bearded hipster one which is wearing casual clothes and a pair of sun glasses, another bearded chubby red-haired, short sleeve shirt wearing with a bottle in one hand and a jacket in the other, the third one has a baseball cap on his head, the cap is turned backwards, t-shirt and white, immaculate sneakers. One of the girls wears a weird backpack with a pair of huge toy glasses on the back of the backpack, under a transparent rain coat. All of them have small backpacks and look like they just started the Camino...in Santiago. Complete rookies, I think. They become the center of my focus. I study them "closely" and construct a good mental case in favor of the fact that they just started the Camino.

In Pontemaceira they stop to take pics of the bridge and the surroundings, they take selfies. I pass them but they pass me afterwards. Pontemaceira looks medieval but it's too little of a location to create a strong impression. We go through a little forest, then through a field and then on the highway. I'm thinking that it's probable that these numbnuts got lost, fact that occurs after they keep on going on the highway instead of following the Camino. No guides in hand, I don't think that they know what they are doing.

After an uphill climb I'm in Chancella and then in

Negreira shortly after. There doesn't seem to be a municipal albergue in the city so I get to Lua which is close by and close to the city center and a Gadis supermarket. Cost: 10 Euros. It's only me, a Polish guy and a Lithuanian. A lot of other people will come one by one afterwards. The Polish guy asks me if I am a German, he can't believe that I'm Romanian. The albergue is not that great, the Internet was not working and it took a technician who came around 5:00 PM to fix the problem. It's almost 14:00 PM so I have to get some bread. I end up going two times at the Gadis supermarket. I spend there 2.51 Euros on: 1.5L of Gaseosa – 0.26 Euro, Tinto wine which comes in a box – 0.59 Euro, bread – 0.50 Euro, bananas – 1.16 Euros. I spend 5.35 Euros on: Asturiana milk – 0.78 Euro, another bread – 0.36 Euro, Salchichon + Chorizo Extra – 1.45 Euros, Queso – 1.28 Euros, Oreos – 1.48 Euros.

I go to the Bazaar Chino which is right next to Gadis and I spend 10 Euros for a 1.5 liters capacity military looking flask – thinking that will help me hydrate on the go, at the moment I'm carrying the bottles on top of my backpack so it's a hustle each time I want to have a drink – and a garlic crusher that I want to give as a gift to my grandma – 2.7 Euros. I also buy a multipurpose "Polar" bandana for 17 Euros from some sports goods shop. I spent quite a lot today. There is not much to do in town or at the albergue.

I bought extra food for tomorrow because it seems that there won't be supermarkets in the small settlements we will be passing through on our way and also at the destination in Olveiroa.

Days 36 & 37, 26 & 27 May, Cee & Finisterre

This is where my journal entries end and I will explain in the following lines why. Day 36 was the longest day in my journey. I started at 7:20 AM from Negreira and got to the albergue in the beautiful town of Cee at about 8:50 PM. I walked all day basically with some short stops from time to time and totaling about 52 kilometers, the longest distance that I've done in a day on the Camino. Needless to say, I was too tired to stay and write at the end of the day like I usually have done. The hospitalero at the albergue in Cee was quite impressed when he heard about my feat, he asked me if I want to go to a restaurant in order to eat something so that he can recommend me one, I said that I'm rather interested in a supermarket, he replies that all the supermarkets close at 9:00 PM. Not having much to eat and being low on supplies I get panicky and ask where can I find one, he says that there is one about 200 meters farther and he gives me directions. I leave all my stuff at the entry of the albergue, I didn't even had time to get to the dormitory, and start running in the direction that he told me. I end up running a distance more than 200 meters because I miss the supermarket, ask a man, run up to a building that turns out not to be a supermarket, turn back and notice where the supermarket was all along and run towards it. I manage to buy my needed supplies just in time.

The morning was cold and a dense fog covered

everything. I passed by a church and a cemetery that were covered in a dense fog, the view made for a good spooky photo that I took. Out of Negreira there is a sign that says Muxia and the Camino seemed to go to Muxia which made me confused because my plan was to go to Finisterre first not Muxia. After a moment of thought and after checking all the informations that I've got I concluded that "I don't know how to head to Finisterre anyway, I might just go to Muxia instead". Turns out that the road doesn't fork into Finisterre and Muxia that early out of Negreira but much later on, some 10 kilometers or so before Cee.

Encountered a couple from Portugal on my way, they told me a bit about Portugal: beautiful places, good people, cheap, secure and so on.

I meet the Lithuanian guy from the albergue again, he is staying on a stone bench and is relaxing, I stop to have a shoes and socks drying session and to eat and drink something – I'm making good use now of my new 1.5 liters canteen.

I don't stop at the albergue in Oliveiroa but choose to go further because I want my last day to Finisterre to be a shorter day, I want to get there at the "end of the Earth" and spend some time along with my thoughts, to reflect on this journey, on my life, what should I do when I came back home and so on. Soon after Oliveiroa I see Hannah and Aqualina from Canada. Well, I think that I saw them only once before in Negreira, they were singing aloud on the streets and walking blissfully. I'm walking on one side of the road and they are walking on the other side when one of them, Hannah, sees me and asks me what I'm doing on that side of the road. I come over to their side of the road and that's how I make acquaintance with them. They start singing again. We talk about various things and it turns out that they know some Romanian to my surprise, they stayed through an au pair program in France at a family, and the family happened to be Romanian. They learned to count in Romanian up to 38 because that's how many times the family's child would jump on the trambouline and would count 1,2,3...38. I start saying unu, doi, trei, patru and the girls continued up to treizeci si opt. Impressive, their Romanian is good. We meet a Korean woman and Aqualina starts saying that she knows some words and expressions in Korean, she shows off her Korean but the Korean woman doesn't understands anything. Me and Hannah go ahead and keep talking while Aqualina and the Korean woman remain behind us. We go through some amazing scenery but I'm oblivious to it, I'm too focused talking to Hannah...I peak an eye at the surrounding scenery and I exclaim "Oh, wow!", she takes a peak at the scenery too and exclaims as well. It's a very scenic valley. On the road we see I live viper staying in the middle of the road and heating its cold blood in the sun. How do I know that it's a viper? I actually read about it some days ago, poisonous snakes have a triangular head shape. At Logoso, I think, there is a small private albergue and all the places are already occupied. The owner says that his sister owns a hotel about one kilometer away on the other side of the valley, it's visible from where we stand. The girls decide to go there so we have to part ways unfortunately. I politely ask the owner to fill my canteen with water knowing that I still have plenty of road ahead. At about 6:30 PM, if I remember correctly I get to a place called "Hospital" on my sheet of paper, it looks like a small restaurant but it's full with people I can hear them from a distance. About one kilometer from this "Hospital" there is the crossroad where the road splits to Muxia and to Cee. After a few hundred meters on the highway the Camino takes a turn and goes through beautiful and wild scenery, soft land and a lot of greenery. All this beauty gives me a sense of peacefulness, there are no more other travelers this late in the day, no cars, only nature and a sun that is starting to slowly set. Beautiful scenery all the way to Cee.

I hoped to see in Cee the mother and daughter team from Germany again but it didn't happened.

I arrive in Finisterre somewhere before 12:00 AM, there are only 16 kilometers from Cee to here after all. It was a pleasant walk, the last kilometers of the road are along the coastline. I find a private albergue to stay at after passing by the public one and not seeing it. There are not many things to do in Finisterre, I try to visit a small fortress but it was closed. I buy some tangerines and some nuts and I proceed towards the "end". The weather is capricious, there are strong winds, it's cloudy and it even starts to rain. When I get to the lighthouse I am a bit surprised, I didn't knew exactly what to expect coming here but in my mind I had this image in which I'm staying all by myself at the edge of a cliff and watching the dramatic scenery and thinking about various things. In reality, there are plenty of tourists here and the place has a touristic vibe to it, there are cars, camper cars, there are tent shops where you can buy various things. I visit the lighthouse, see the pillar which indicates kilometer zero, go at the edge of the cliff and climb down as far as I can while navigating between people, boulders and charred remains of clothes, shoes and other objects that the peregrinos chose to burn during their Camino ritual. I go up the cliff, find a more secluded spot and do my thinking.

I hoped to see the Canadian girls again, looked for them around Cee but this didn't happened either, maybe they went to Muxia instead, who knows.

I don't write anything today too, I don't feel like it, I'm considering this day as a "vacation" day. I buy some wine and drink it while sitting alone in my room at the albergue and listening to The End by The Doors.
"This is the end, beautiful friend
This is the end, my only friend, the end."

Tomorrow I will get the bus to Santiago and from there another bus to Porto.

Takeaways for the Camino traveler

A light backpack is recommended, mine had about 10 kilograms more or less and was the source of a lot of ache.

There is no need to carry more than food rations for a day or two. Water is quite abundant on the road and especially in the first stages, there is no need to carry more than 1-1.5 liters of water at a time.

Sundays are always problematic when it comes to getting food because all of the big supermarkets are close. However, there might be the odd little shop that it's open. Catholic Holy Days are also problematic because everything is closed.

Pack warm and waterproof clothes. It's colder and wetter in the North of Spain than in the rest of the country.

Cushioned running shoes seem to work well given the terrain, I've seen plenty of people wearing them and going over rocky roads with no problems. Waterproof trekking shoes should also work.

If you get lost you might want to check out the nearest church, the Camino usually goes through religious points of interest like churches, cathedrals, monasteries and even cemeteries.

Tourism Information Centers are usually not far

from the Camino and the information and maps that you can get for free can be of great help. They are usually closed on Mondays.

Having a basic understanding of Spanish is recommended. Knowing basic keywords can help you formulate and ask questions and having a basic understanding of the language helps you to extract information from the people. The Spanish people are quite helpful and they are usually happy to see you speak or at least try to speak their language.

Having a guide book helps but is not necessarily a must. There are lots of people with guides and you can just ask them for various information, sometimes you don't even have to ask them, they will just say it, people like helping other people and sharing knowledge.

Earplugs and eye masks can make the difference between a good sleep and a bad sleep.

Take care of your feet. Take the right shoes. Make sure that your feet, your socks and your shoes are dry. Light sandals are great for walking in the albergues and for short distances at the end of the day. I didn't used any cremes, or some specific products for taking care of the feet so I can't recommend any. I've seen many people using various products but I preferred to stay with the natural way of healing and sometimes only used a needle to puncture and dry my blisters. I used anti-blister socks but it seems that they weren't that effective since my feet ended up covered in plenty of blisters anyway.

About the Author

When I'm not writing, traveling or running I'm usually busy building things. I'm a software developer by trade and currently attempting to succeed as an entrepreneur.

Thanks for reading, I hope that you enjoyed it. If you have questions or suggestions please contact me at stefan@stefantesoi.com or through my website http://stefantesoi.com